Eyewitness
RELIGION

Date: 9/4/12

*The soul is like a charioteer
with two horses, one fine
and good and noble,
and the other the opposite*

PLATO IN *PHAEDRUS* (ADAPTED)

The Greek
deities Eros,
Aphrodite, and Pan

Gemstone inscri[...]
with verse fr[...]
the Qu[...]

Buddha head

*The mind is wavering and restless…
let the wise straighten their minds
as makers of arrows make their
arrows straight*

GAUTAMA THE BUDDHA (ADAPTED)

*To God belongs the kingdom of the
heavens and of the Earth; and God
is powerful over everything*

QUR'AN IV

*I am all that has ever been,
I am all that is,
I am all that ever shall be,
yet never have mortal eyes
perceived me as I am*

SONG TO THE EGYPTIAN MOTHER GODDESS NEIT

Egyptian Ankh

Christian plaque
showing Christ
on the cross

*I have been born again and again,
from time to time… To protect
the righteous, to destroy the wicked,
and to establish the kingdom of God,
I am reborn from age to age*

KRISHNA IN THE *BHAGAVAD GITA* IV

*Jesus Christ is the
same yesterday and
today and forever*

HEBREWS 13:8

Statue of Hindu
avatar Krishna

Eyewitness
RELIGION

Written by
MYRTLE LANGLEY

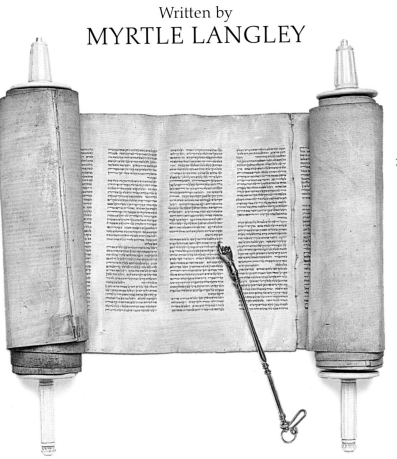

A Jewish
Torah scroll

God said to Moses, "I AM WHO I AM.
This is what you are to say to the Israelites:
'I AM has sent me to you'"

EXODUS 3: 14

DK Publishing

LONDON, NEW YORK,
MELBOURNE, MUNICH, and DELHI

Project editor David Pickering
Art editor Sharon Spencer
Managing editor Gillian Denton
Managing art editor Julia Harris
Production Charlotte Trail
Picture research Kathy Lockley
Researcher Julie Ferris
Special photography Ellen Howden,
Andy Crawford, Geoff Dann,
Ray Moller, and Gary Ombler

REVISED EDITION
Revised by Philip Wilkinson

DK INDIA
Project editor Nidhi Sharma
Project art editor Rajnish Kashyap
Editor Pallavi Singh
Designer Honlung Zach Ragui
Managing editor Saloni Talwar
Managing art editor Romi Chakraborty
DTP designer Tarun Sharma
Picture researcher Sumedha Chopra

DK UK
Senior editor Rob Houston
Senior art editor Philip Letsu
Production editor Adam Stoneham
Publisher Andrew Macintyre

DK US
US editor Margaret Parrish
Editorial director Nancy Ellwood

This revised edition published in the United States in 2012
by DK Publishing, 375 Hudson Street, New York, New York 10014
First published in the United States in 1996

10 9 8 7 6 5 4 3 2 1

001—183546—July/12

DK books are available at special discounts when purchased in bulk for sales
promotions, premiums, fundraising, or educational use. For details, contact:
DK Publishing Special Markets 375 Hudson Street, New York, New York 10014
SpecialSales@dk.com

A catalog record for this book is available from the Library of Congress.
ISBN: 978-0-7566-9079-3 (Hardback)
ISBN: 978-0-7566-9080-9 (Libraray binding)

Color reproduction by Colourscan, Singapore
Printed and bound in China by Toppan Printing Co. (Shenzhen) Ltd.

Discover more at
www.dk.com

Bishop's miter

Islamic tile

Tile with writing from the Qur'an

Christian rosary
used in prayer

Hindu goddess Durga

Reclining
Buddha

Jewish Seder plate
for Passover

Tibetan
prayer
wheel

Contents

Introduction

When, as tiny babies, we first enter this world, we have no experience; we know no words; our minds are not filled with thoughts and ideas. We simply exist, aware only of our immediate surroundings and secure in the love of our parents. As we grow older we become aware of ourselves and our wider surroundings; we learn to communicate through speech as well as in other ways. Our minds and spirits are opened up to thoughts and ideas, experience and reflection. Questions are asked. Answers are sought. Who am I? Why is the world as it is? Why do people die? Why isn't everybody happy? What is God like? Does God really exist? The world's religions and their founders have asked these questions and given their own very different and yet at the same time very similar answers. "Know yourself." "Know God." These two ideas sum up the religious search and at the same time help us to find again the peace and happiness we knew as children.

The religious quest

LIGHT OF LIFE
Since ancient times, people have recognized that life on Earth depends on the Sun. Many have visualized God as light and life, and have used the Sun as a symbol for God.

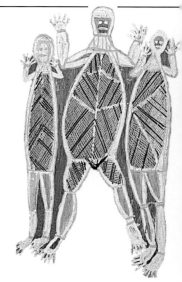

CREATION STORY
This Australian bark painting shows an Aboriginal ancestral group from the Dreamtime, a time when the landscape received its present form. In many religions, moral laws are rooted in beliefs about creation, or beliefs about ancestors.

THE WORLD CAN BE an uncomfortable place to live in as well as a cause for excitement and wonder. Life itself can be both puzzling and exhilarating. A person may feel very much alone although surrounded by others. To a very great extent, existence and the universe remain a mystery. So, from the earliest times humankind has set out on a religious quest or spiritual search, so that life and death may take on some meaning and significance.

Out of this search, the world's religions have emerged. Broadly speaking, there are two main traditions. One accepts the essential goodness of the physical world but tries to change parts of it that are wrong or broken. The other says that reality is essentially spiritual, and seeks to release the soul from an endless round of birth, death, and rebirth in the material world. Religions have several different dimensions. They teach people how to live, and tell myths—stories about gods and creation, which help to explain life. They offer their followers systems of ideas and beliefs, rituals, and ceremonies that bring people together, social organizations to belong to, and the possibility of experiencing a greater reality.

> *Religion is not alien to us…*
> *It is always within us: with*
> *some consciously;*
> *with others, unconsciously.*
> *But it is always there*
>
> MAHATMA GANDHI

Uluru (previously known as Ayers Rock)

REACHING UPWARD
The seven terraces of the great Buddhist monument of Borobudur in Indonesia are lined with scenes of the Buddha's spiritual progress, carved in stone. As pilgrims walk around and upward, they learn about how to follow his example. At the top is an empty, bell-shaped dome, perhaps inviting the presence of the Buddha and his wisdom. Many religions use architecture, sculpture, and the other arts to convey their ideas.

LIFE AND DEATH
Death comes to everyone. It is both welcomed and feared. Yet, many people see indications that this life is not the only one and death is not the end. They imagine another life where wrongs will be righted. Often, in dreams, people may look at themselves from outside their own bodies. On visiting new places, they feel sure that they have been there before. Some believe that the soul is endlessly reborn in different bodies, others that soul and body are reunited after death. Tombs and funeral rituals may be seen as part of the preparation for the next life.

CLEANSING AND HEALING
Water is essential to life, so springs and rivers have long featured in religion as symbols of spiritual life and centers of pilgrimage. Here, in the river Ganges, India, people drink of the holy water or bathe in it for healing and cleansing.

The rock is 1,142 ft (348 m) high, 4 miles (6 km) long, and 1.3 miles (2 km) wide

You have made us for Yourself, and our hearts are restless until they rest in You

AUGUSTINE OF HIPPO

Islamic tombstone

HOLY MOUNTAIN
This vast stone outcrop called Uluru, in Australia, is of great spiritual significance to its Aboriginal custodians. Close relationships with the Earth and nature are at the heart of all Aboriginal beliefs and customs. The landscape itself is seen as full of spiritual meaning. Several other religions include similar beliefs, and a number of mountains around the world are considered holy. Some are seen as places where gods live.

The Willendorf Venus, an Earth goddess figure

There are many sacred caves in the lower parts of the rock

FERTILITY AND THE MOTHER GODDESS
Life depends on the fertility of the Earth, together with light and water from heaven. The Sun god and Earth goddess have often been pictured as coming together to produce life. Lesser gods, such as Thunder and Rain, and human workers, make sure the land is fertile. It is likely that worship of the "Mother goddess"— associated with springtime and harvest, sowing and reaping, and the bearing of children—is an early, if not the earliest, religious idea.

7

Life and death in Egypt

THE ANCIENT EGYPTIANS had many gods. The chief of them all was the Sun god, who was worshiped in many different forms, and was seen as responsible for all creation. The other gods each had charge of a different area of life. Believing that all events were controlled by the gods, Egyptians made many offerings to try to keep them happy, hoping that the gods would bless them. They tried to lead good lives so as to be ready for the judgment of the god Osiris, who ruled the heavenly kingdom where Egyptians wished to live after death. They pictured this kingdom as a perfect version of Egypt, called "The Field of Reeds." To get there, the dead had to make a difficult journey through the underworld, which was called Duat. If they managed to pass Duat's monsters and lakes of fire, they faced judgment by Osiris in the Hall of Two Truths.

SIGN OF LIFE
Only gods, kings, and queens were allowed to carry the ankh, the sign of life. It showed that they had the power to give life, or take it away.

EYE OF HORUS
Wadjet eye amulets were place on mummies to protect them. wadjet eye represented the ey that the sky god Horus lost fighting the evil Seth, god o chaos and disorder, for the thro of Egypt. Magically restored, acquired healing properties, a symbolized the victory of god over evil. It was said to protec anything behind it.

Outer coffin of Pasenhor, one of many Libyans who settled in Egypt

Symbols were painted on mummy cases to help on the voyage to the afterlife

A HOME FOR THE SPIRIT
The Egyptians prepared for the afterlife in several ways. They mummified the bodies of the dead to make them last forever, so that a dead person's spirit would always have a home. They also filled their tombs with magical protection to help them to survive the dangerous journey across Duat, and with food and equipment they might need.

THE PLACE OF JUDGMENT
If the dead managed to cross Duat, they had to pass a final test, set in the Hall of Two Truths. The dead person's heart was weighed in the balance against the Feather of Truth, symbol of Ma'at, goddess of order, truth, and justice, to see if it was heavy with sin. In this picture, the person passes the test and is presented to Osiris. Had he failed, the monster Ammit would have eaten his heart.

The dead person is led by the jackal-headed god Anubis

The god Thoth records the result

Ammit, devourer of the dead

The Feather of Truth

The dead person's heart is in one scale

REBIRTH

Many religions have a belief in rebirth, also called new birth or second birth. This can mean passing from childhood to adulthood, awakening to spiritual life, or moving from death to life. It is often symbolized by passing through water or, as in Egypt, by leaving the grave and meeting the god of rebirth.

MAGIC SPELLS
The *Book of the Dead* is a scroll (roll) of papyrus containing a collection of magic spells. Each spell was a prayer or a plea from the dead person meant to help on the voyage through Duat to the heavenly afterlife. This statue of Osiris has a hidden compartment where the scroll was kept.

Shabti figures

Roll of papyrus

Secret compartment

O you living upon Earth, who love life and hate death…

INSCRIPTION ON EGYPTIAN TOMB

GOD OF REBIRTH
Osiris, god of rebirth, judged people's souls in the afterlife. He was said to have triumphed over death, and every Egyptian wanted to follow his example. This statue of him would have been placed in a tomb or a temple.

Box containing the shabti figures shows gods and a priestess

Osiris presides over judgment

The guardian goddesses—Isis, wife of Osiris, and Nephthys, her sister

WORKER FIGURES
The Egyptians believed that after death Osiris might order them to work in the fields in his heavenly land. So rich people provided their mummies with shabtis, carved figures who would spring to life and do their work for them in the afterlife.

The four Sons of Horus, guardians of the vital organs, standing on a lotus flower

Gods of the Nile

Bronze statuette of Bastet, Saqqara

PTAH
Worshiped especially at Memphis, Ptah was a creator god. According to one account, he made the cosmos by first thinking about it and then speaking it into existence. Ptah was also the god of sculptors and carvers, and his shrine was near their limestone quarries close to the city.

In addition to presiding over the journey from life to death, the gods of ancient Egypt also controlled the daily life of the people. This life centered on the Nile River, which gave the Egyptians their main transportation route and a rich source of fish and other food. When it flooded annually, it brought rich silt to its banks that helped their crops grow. The Egyptians believed that their gods and goddesses ruled the Nile and the land on its banks. The deities did this by bringing life into being, by controlling the floods, and by protecting the people from fierce river creatures. These gods and goddesses lived by the banks and often took the form of creatures who lived there, such as cows, cats, beetles, and crocodiles.

BASTET
The daughter of the Su[n] god, the cat-goddess Bas[tet] was the defender of h[er] father and the pharao[h,] fearlessly attacking the[ir] enemies. She also had [a] peaceful side, using he[r] power to help the Sun g[od] ripen the crops. Her ma[in] temple was at Bubasti[s,] which housed figures [of] her and mummified ca[ts] dedicated to her.

An ancient statue of the ram god Khnum

KHEPRI
The Sun god took many forms. One form was Khepri, the scarab beetle. Just as a real scarab beetle rolled a ball of dung, Khepri pushed the disk of the Sun across the sky until nighttime, when the disk vanished into the body of Nut, goddess of the night. The Egyptians often made seals and jewelry in the form of a scarab beetle.

A gold scarab brooch from the tomb of Tutankhamen, studded with semiprecious stones

KHNUM
With the body of a man and the head of a ram, Khnum was one of the most powerful gods of the Nile. He controlled the river's cataracts, instructing another god, Hapy, to emerge from his cavern each year and cause the river to flood and spread fertile mud over its banks. A skilled craftworker, Khnum used some of this mud to create life-forms, including human beings, which he molded on his potter's wheel.

Temple of Hathor at Dendera, Nile valley

HATHOR
Worshiped at her temple at Dendera, Hatho[r] was the goddess of love, beauty, fertility, and motherhood. She sometimes took the form [of] a cow that lived among the papyrus marshe[s] on the fertile banks of the Nile and produce[d] milk for the pharaoh. However, she also appeared as a beautiful young woman, whose head topped each of the columns of her temple.

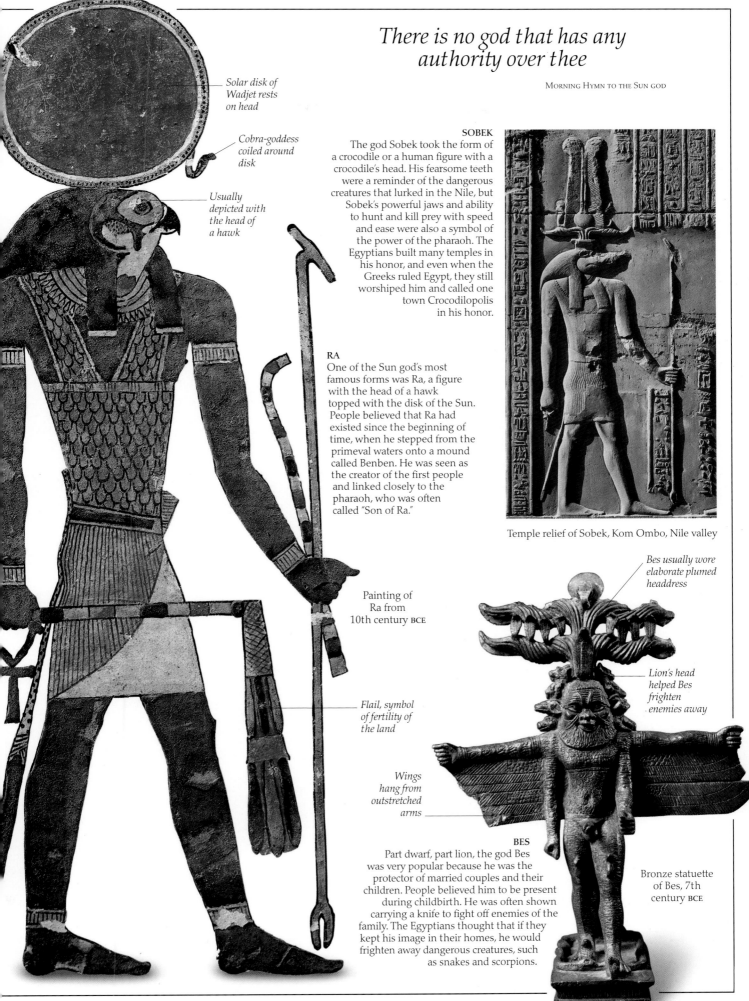

Solar disk of
Wadjet rests
on head

Cobra-goddess
coiled around
disk

Usually
depicted with
the head of
a hawk

SOBEK

The god Sobek took the form of a crocodile or a human figure with a crocodile's head. His fearsome teeth were a reminder of the dangerous creatures that lurked in the Nile, but Sobek's powerful jaws and ability to hunt and kill prey with speed and ease were also a symbol of the power of the pharaoh. The Egyptians built many temples in his honor, and even when the Greeks ruled Egypt, they still worshiped him and called one town Crocodilopolis in his honor.

RA

One of the Sun god's most famous forms was Ra, a figure with the head of a hawk topped with the disk of the Sun. People believed that Ra had existed since the beginning of time, when he stepped from the primeval waters onto a mound called Benben. He was seen as the creator of the first people and linked closely to the pharaoh, who was often called "Son of Ra."

Temple relief of Sobek, Kom Ombo, Nile valley

Bes usually wore
elaborate plumed
headdress

Lion's head
helped Bes
frighten
enemies away

Painting of
Ra from
10th century BCE

Flail, symbol
of fertility of
the land

Wings
hang from
outstretched
arms

BES

Part dwarf, part lion, the god Bes was very popular because he was the protector of married couples and their children. People believed him to be present during childbirth. He was often shown carrying a knife to fight off enemies of the family. The Egyptians thought that if they kept his image in their homes, he would frighten away dangerous creatures, such as snakes and scorpions.

Bronze statuette
of Bes, 7th
century BCE

Gods and nature in Greece

IN ANCIENT GREECE, nature was considered to hold the power of life and was therefore sacred. A mountain was the sky god's throne—the worshipers climbed it to pray for rain, not to admire the view. Every tree had its own spirit— the oak was sacred to Zeus, the olive to Athena, the laurel to Apollo, and the myrtle to Aphrodite. Groves were considered especially holy and were used as places of refuge. Each spring also had its nymph, each river its god, and the sea was home to many deities and spirits. Every area of life was overseen by a deity. People could choose the god they thought would help them best. The gods intervened in human life as and when they chose, helping those they liked, and harming others.

HUNTER AND MOTHER
Artemis was the goddess of hunting and the Moon. At Ephesus, she was worshiped with the Great Mother, an ancient goddess linked with the Earth and fertility.

THE PARTHENON
Built between 447 and 432 BCE by the [c...] leader, Pericles, the Parthenon stood on [...] highest point of the Acropolis in Athen[s...] was dedicated to the goddess Athena a[...] housed a huge gold and ivory statue of [...]

Eros, Aphrodite's son, also a god of love

Aphrodite appears as a graceful young woman

Pan, a wild nature god, has goat's legs and ears

APOLLO
Apollo, brother of Artemis, was th[e] model of youthful strength and beauty. A powerful god, he was associated with the Sun, light, prophecy, and healing, but if he w[as] angry, his arrows could cause plag[ue.]

The goose is a symbol of Aphrodite

GODDESS OF LOVE
Aphrodite was the goddess of love and beauty. She was also called the "foam-born" because she was said to have risen from the sea when it was sprinkled with the seed and blood of ancient, defeated gods. On this mirror case, she is playing the ancient game of knucklebones with the wild, goatlike nature god, Pan.

EARTH MOTHER
Demeter was the goddess of the harvest. It was said that when her daughter Persephone was stolen by Pluto, king of Hades (the underworld), her sorrow made the crops stop growing. Persephone was released, on the condition that she had eaten nothing in Hades. In fact, she had eaten six pomegranate seeds, so had to stay in Hades for six months each year. This story explained why we have winter and spring.

Demeter and Persephone sit side by side in this terra-cotta figure, probabl[y] holding the rei[ns] of an ox-cart

Zeus, king of
the gods

Aegeus, king
of Athens,
consulting
the oracle

THE DELPHIC ORACLE
In ancient Greece, people consulted the gods
on major decisions. The most important place to
visit for this was the shrine of Apollo at Delphi.
His priestess, or the oracle, went into a trance,
uttering strange sounds that were interpreted by
priests. Often, even the priest's interpretations
could be hard for those consulting the oracle
to understand.

NG OF THE GODS
us was the greatest of
gods. He ruled the Earth
d the sky. His symbol was the
nderbolt, with which he handed
justice, violently, on Earth and in heaven.
brothers, Poseidon and Hades, ruled the
and the underworld, respectively. Zeus married his sister
ra, and fathered countless gods, demigods, and mortals by
and many others. In art or sculpture, Zeus is usually shown
a middle-aged, bearded man of great power and dignity.

WISE WARRIOR
Athena was the goddess of
wisdom, including literature,
philosophy, and the arts, and a
war goddess as well. She was
also patron of the city of Athens.
Her symbols were the owl and
the olive tree. Each city had a
patron deity, who was particularly
honored and looked up to for help,
especially in times of trouble.

Greek gods of life

ARES
In Crete, worshipers made sacrifices to Ares, god of war and to his beloved Aphrodite, the goddess of love, both seen here in this fresco at Pompeii, Italy. People believed that both deities could create trouble if they were not appeased with sacrifices. They especially feared Ares because of his violent nature, his tendency to go into a frenzy, and the way he would stir up rivalries. In Athens, people saw him as a protector of young soldiers.

THE ANCIENT GREEKS believed in many gods and goddesses who controlled specific aspects of life on Earth. The Greeks believed that these deities would favor them if they made offerings, or sacrifices. Some of these deities, such as Hephaestus, god of craftworkers and blacksmiths, were worshiped mainly by people who belonged to these professions. Others had shrines in certain towns or cities, where they had a large local following and people regularly held festivals in their honor. Some deities, such as Hestia, goddess of the hearth, had devotees all over Greece.

Clay statue of Eros at Myrina, Greece 300–200

EROS
The god of romantic love, Eros took the shape of a winged boy, as seen in this statue. Usually armed with a bow, Eros would shoot an arrow at someone—either a human or a deity—and the victim fell in love. There were many shrines dedicated to Eros, including some at gymnasia, where people worshiped him as god of physical beauty.

Asclepius with his staff and snake

HEPHAESTUS
The hero Achilles used armor made specially for him by Hephaestus, god of fire, blacksmiths, sculptors, and artisans. This 1st century CE plate shows him wearing it. Hephaestus used his supernatural powers to create all kinds of amazing objects, such as mechanical devices and servants made of gold, and he could also manufacture thunderbolts. His temple at Athens was in the part of the city where metalworkers and other craftsmen had their workshops.

ASCLEPIUS
Asclepius was the Greek god of healing. Statues of the god show him with his staff, around which a snake coils. The staff and snake have become worldwide symbols of medicine. The most important sanctuaries of Asclepius were on the Greek island of Kos, where there was a medical school, and at Epidaurus. Many sick people visited Epidaurus, where they slept in a special area of the sanctuary, hoping to dream that they were healed and to wake up cured.

HESTIA
Hestia was goddess of the hearth, which was the symbol of both the home and the family. Every household left offerings to the goddess by the hearth in her honor. Athens also had a special building where a fire dedicated to Hestia was kept burning. When the Athenians founded a new colony, they took fire from this hearth and used it to light a new fire for the colony.

he holy race of gods...
ons of starry Heaven
and Earth

HESIOD, THEOGONY

PAN

Half man, half goat, Pan was the god of shepherds and their flocks. Pan fell in love with several nymphs in turn, each of whom spurned his love. When the nymph Syrinx ran away from him, he turned her into a reed, from which he made his musical instrument, the syrinx, or panpipes. He also transformed the nymph Pitys into a pine tree, and the nymph Echo into a voice that could only repeat what people said to it.

Athena with
her shield

Aphrodite,
goddess of love

Hera,
goddess of
marriage

Temple of Poseidon,
Cape Sounion, near Athens

Mosaic detail
of Hera,
Athena, and
Aphrodite,
from Antioch
(modern
Antakya,
Turkey)

POSEIDON

One of the most ancient and powerful of all the Greek deities, Poseidon was the god of the sea, earthquakes, and horses. People associated him especially with storms and mishaps at sea, and sailors made a sacrifice to him before going on a voyage. Many temples on coastal sites, such as the one at Sounion on mainland Greece, were built in his honor, but people also worshiped him inland at sites including streams and springs.

DIONYSUS

The god of wine, drunkenness, and the theater, Dionysus was one of the most unpredictable of deities. Stories of his exploits tell of how he traveled around in a kind of drunken ecstasy, accompanied by satyrs (creatures that combined human form with some animal feature, such as the legs of a goat) and female followers called maenads. There were many festivals in honor of Dionysus, featuring noisy processions and dramatic performances.

Satyr

Maenad

Dionysus

Vase showing Dionysus with
maenads and satyrs, 525 BCE

HERA

The wife of Zeus, Hera was the goddess of marriage. Worshipers honored her during rites that took place before weddings. She was also honored as a protector of certain Greek cities. Famous for her serene good looks, Hera, along with Aphrodite and Athena, was among the three most beautiful goddesses. When Eris offered a golden apple as the prize for the fairest, the handsome hero Paris had to choose between the three: he awarded the apple to Aphrodite. As a result, Hera and Athena vowed vengeance on him.

Ancient Norse religion

THE ANCIENT INHABITANTS of Norway, Sweden, and Denmark developed a complex religion involving many gods and goddesses. Their deities lived in a mythical land called Asgard, ruled by their king, Odin. He was one of the most widely worshiped of the Norse gods, along with Thor and Frey—temples sometimes had statues of all three. The Vikings believed that the gods often influenced the lives of men and women, intervening both in their daily lives and in momentous events, such as battles. So the people tried to keep the gods happy by worshiping them, honoring them, and carrying amulets bearing their images or symbols. They also looked forward to a terrible time when there would be a worldwide battle called Ragnarok, when the gods, humans, and the entire Earth would be destroyed.

FREY
Frey was the most important god of fertility. People believed that he controlled both the Sun and the rain. The Vikings prayed to him for good weather and plentiful crops, so that everyone would be well fed. Frey was pictured as a man with a pointed chin, as shown in this statuette from Sweden.

Twisted pattern reminds of the coils of Midgard Serpent

Loki's wife Sigyn catches the venom

LOKI
The trickster god Loki helped oth[er] gods, but could also turn against them. He was the father of three of the gods' most feared enemies— the great wolf Fenrir, the venomo[us] Midgard Serpent, and Hel, godde[ss] the Underworld. Loki's tricks brou[ght] about the death of Odin's virtuou[s] son Baldr, and as punishment, the gods bound him to a rock and let [a] serpent's venom drip into his mou[th]. His faithful wife caught the poiso[n] in a cup, but her cup overflowed a[nd] venom continued to drip.

Iron chains, made from the sinews of his son

Plant used as a herbal medicine

The punishment of Loki

Staring eyes—a common design on amulets

Decorative gold panel

Amulet in the shape of Thor's hammer

FRIGG
The wife of Odin, Frigg was a beautiful goddess who was sometimes thought to be Freyja— their names have similar meanings, "woman" and "lady." She often joined her husband in influencing human affairs and sometimes quarreled with him. Images of her are rare, but people thought that she was present in the wildflower Lady's bedstraw (*Galium verum*), which they called Frigg's grass.

Lady's bedstraw

THOR
The thunder god Thor, the mightiest of the Norse gods, was a fearsome figure with a red beard, piercing eyes, and a huge appetite. His main weapon was his hammer, which he used to slay giants and to make the sound of the thunder. Thor was one of the most popular gods, and some people wore a brooch or amulet shaped like a hammer to ensure that he would protect them.

FREYJA
Frey's sister, Freyja was the most popular goddess. She was mainly worshiped for her power of love and beauty, and some accounts of her say that she had many lovers. She also had a darker side, going into battle alongside the god [of] Odin and claiming many victims. S[he] was also believed to have a husba[nd] named Od, who left her. She is sa[id] to have gone in search for him [in] a chariot pulled by a pair of c[ats].

ODIN

The god Odin was the king of Norse deities and had a huge following. His high seat, or dwelling place, Hliðskjálf, was in Asgard—one of the nine worlds of the Norse gods. He was the god of war, victory, wisdom, poetry, and death. He was the father of most of the other gods, and, together with his brothers, Vili and Ve, created the first humans. His priests carried ceremonial swords and spears as a reminder that Odin sometimes intervened in human battles.

Pair of spears

Sword

Bronze figure of a priest of Odin wearing a helmet, found in a 9th-century grave in Uppland, Sweden

Ornate patterns depict mythical beast

The Jelling Stone

Prow in the shape of a coiled snake

CONVERSION TO CHRISTIANITY

During the 10th century, under the influence of the Christian countries around them, the Vikings began to convert to Christianity. One of the first leaders to convert was Harald Bluetooth, king of Denmark, who became a Christian in the 960s. At the grave site of his parents in Jelling, Denmark, he built a church and reburied his parents inside. He had this stone carved as a memorial to them.

A champion who enters Odin's dwelling-place does not bemoan his death

DEATH-SONG OF RAGNAR IOTHBROK

[BU]RIAL SITE

[Th]e Vikings believed in an afterlife, [an]d so they buried their dead with [them?]. It was common to bury the dead [wit]h grave goods—items they could [use] in the next world. The graves of [resp]ected men and women were [met]iculously laid out, like these near [Lind]borg, Denmark, where the plots are [ma]rked with stones. This burial site [has] more than 600 graves dating back [to t]he Iron Age (400–800 CE) and the [Vik]ing period (800–1085 CE).

[ra]ck where [the] oars were stacked

Overlapping planks of oak

SHIP BURIAL

When a Viking king or queen died, their followers sometimes buried them in their ship, with a large collection of grave goods and sometimes even the sacrificed bodies of servants. One of these ship burials at Oseberg, Norway, contained the skeletons of two women and a large collection of their belongings, including sleighs, a cart, furniture, and clothing. The magnificent ship is now on display in a museum in Oslo. Recent research has shown that the ship was capable of sailing in open seas.

Oseberg ship

Native religions

THE POWER OF LIFE
There is a widespread belief among followers of native religions that all living things are invested with mana (spiritual power). Throughout the Pacific islands of Polynesia the arts, especially wood carving, were used to represent gods, nature spirits, and the spirits of the ancestors, and to provide "vehicles" (material "homes") for their mana. This carving, from the Cook Islands, is of a god associated with canoe-making and with bringing good luck to fishermen.
The same gods are found repeatedly among the many different peoples of Polynesia, sometimes under different names.

IN SOME PARTS of the world, people follow native religions—those that have grown up in those places and been handed down by word of mouth from one generation to another for thousands of years. There are still many followers of these religions in Africa, the Americas, and Oceania. For them, all of life is religious and nothing takes place outside a spiritual framework. They look to the spiritual world for blessing. Those who live along Africa's Rift Valley, on the plains of the Americas, or on Pacific islands, associate God with the Sun and sky, and organize their lesser gods to mirror their own societies. The Maasai of East Africa worship One God linked with the Sun, while the Yoruba people of Nigeria worship a High God who rules over many lesser gods. Those living in rainforests, or in densely settled areas, worship the spirits of nature and give great respect to their ancestors.

HEALING AND HARM
Followers of native religions believe that sickness can be caused by the living or the dead. If spirits of ancestors are not worshiped, they may strike, or if the living are offended, they can cast a spell. Healers use either spiritual powers or medicine to cure their patients.

Afric
heal
cha
neck

SACRIFICE

From the earliest times, sacrifice has been offered to ancestors, spirits, or gods, to avert their anger, express thanks, or for other reasons. It has often required the laying down of life, usually of animals, such as cattle and sheep. Sometimes worshipers sacrifice by giving up pleasures or possessions.

Doll made from stick, beeswax, beads, hide

Two fertility dolls from Angola, in Southwest Africa (center and right)

OSHUN SHRI
Among the Yoruba, the ma goddess is Oshun, the ri goddess. It is said that the wo of the male gods was faili until she joined them. Wom worship her if they wish become pregnant, or to protected from disea

Central part of doll made from corn cob

Fertility doll from Cameroon, in West Africa

FERTILE EAR
Many peop look to the spir and the ancesto to give them t Sun, rain, and fert soil that they nee They also pray to spiri ancestors, and Mother Ear to make their women fertile and bring them lar families. In some societies, girls and young women ca around fertility dolls such as these to make them ferti

18

The metal acts like a mirror to reflect back any evil that threatens the ancestor

Each of the three main figures carries signs of leadership: a knife, tusk, and elaborate headdress

These heads may represent family slaves

Kota guardian figure made of wood covered in brass

GUARDIAN FIGURE
Some societies believe that the physical remains of important people can hold something of the power those people held in their lifetimes. Among the Kota people of Gabon, the skulls and bones of important ancestors are kept in baskets in a special hut and offerings are made to them. Guardian figures such as this are placed on such baskets to protect the ancestors' remains from evil forces.

Those who are dead are never gone

AFRICAN PROVERB

The three figures would originally have worn cloth wraps over their legs

ANCESTRAL SCREEN
It is believed that ancestors will protect and guide living relatives who honor them. Among the Kalabari people of Nigeria, screens such as this one were placed behind altars where descendants made offerings to the spirit of the ancestor depicted on the screen. On this screen, the central figure is the head of a prosperous trading house. He is standing with two sons or attendants.

Sande
initiation
mask

Rituals of life

RITUALS OF LIFE play a major role in native religions. They are largely of two kinds—"rites of passage" and "rites of affliction." Rites of passage take place at important moments of a person's passage through life, such as birth, puberty, marriage, divorce, and death. Rites of affliction arise at times of crisis such as illness or disaster. The rituals are usually divided into three stages— separation from the old, transition, and inclusion into the new. For example, young people at puberty may be separated from society (and, symbolically, from childhood), then instructed on how to be adults, and then incorporated back into society as full adult members of their communities. In some societies, the rituals may be performed by priests, in others by ritual leaders, shamans, or healers.

FUNERAL DANCE
Funeral rites are important in nat
religions. Among the Dogon peo
of West Africa they are occasion
for elaborate public dances (abov
accompanied by chants in a secr
language. The rite retells the Dog
myth of how death entered the
world through the disobedience
young men. The Awa masked
society also helps to preserve oth
popular Dogon myths. In this
image, the dancers are wearing
skirts dyed in red, the color
associated with death.

ELEPHANT SPIRIT MASK
Many African peoples make masks, mainly to represent the spirits when these are called on to be present at ceremonies. Some have human features, others those of animals. They are not made to look realistic. Instead, traditional symbolic styles are followed, which are understood by ritual experts who interpret for the people. For instance, the elephant spirit is a symbol of ugliness. This elephant spirit mask was made by the Igbo people of Nigeria.

This mask is worn on top of the head

INITIATION MASK
Among the Mende people of West Africa, young girls are initiated into the Sande society, a women's secret society, at puberty. Elders instruct them in domestic and craft skills and prepare them for marriage and motherhood. As part of the initiation, a masked dance, or masquerade, is held. This gives people a chance to express themselves through a ceremony that unites them. Sande masks represent power, emotion, and womanly qualities. They symbolically express the Mende ideal of female beauty.

There is no distinction between religion and the rest of life. All of life is religious

AFRICAN SAYING

INITIATION MASK
Masks can represent important ancestors. This royal initiation mask comes from the Kuba kingdom in the Democratic Republic of the Congo. It represents the son of the first divine king. Masks play an important role in initiation ceremonies. Other Kuba masks, made to look like spirits, were worn by chiefs to enforce discipline.

SPIRITS AND HEALING
For the Yoruba people, all forces which affect people, good or bad, are seen as coming from the spirits. For example, there are spirits of technology, such as the automobile, and spirits of illnesses. Sometimes the Yoruba spirits, such as the smallpox spirit above, are represented by images and are invoked (called on) for healing and blessing.

The use of cowrie shells in decoration is widespread and usually symbolizes fertility

SUMMONING THE SPIRITS
Among the original peoples of the far north of North America and Asia, those who get in touch with the spirit world are known as "shamans." Shamans' masks, such as this Alaskan one, are worn at festivals, and at rituals of healing and of divination (seeing into the future).

ur oval faces, each nked by a pair of raised hands, round the central e of the Sun

WINTER FESTIVAL
During their winter ceremony, the Bella Coola people of western Canada performed dances taught to them by the spirits of the sky. Wearing masks representing the spirits, the dancers acted out with great drama the central stories of their people's beliefs. This mask with its spherical face represents the spirit of the Sun.

Encircling wood hoops once completely bound with fur

21

The Hindu way

To BE A HINDU is to be born a Hindu, and then to follow a certain way of life. The word "Hindu" comes from "Hind," the old Persian word for India, and Hinduism originally meant the religion of the people of India. With no founder and no creed, it has evolved over time. As we know it today, it can be compared to a great, deep river into which, over a period of more than 3,000 years, many streams have flowed. The streams are the beliefs and practices of the numerous ethnic groups and cultures of the Indian subcontinent. Hinduism has many gods yet, for some Hindus, there is an impersonal "Absolute" behind them all, called Brahman, creator of the universe. Brahman "unfolds" into the Trimurti, the holy trinity made up of Brahma, Vishnu, and Shiva. Brahma is the creator, Vishnu the great preserver, and Shiva the destroyer but also the re-creator. Hindus everywhere believe in reincarnation, the individual soul born again in another body. Life flows on through many existences, from birth through death to rebirth. If people are good in one life, they will be rewarded by being well born in their next life.

The all-seeing Brahma has four heads, of which the sculpture shows three

BRAHMA THE CREATOR
Brahma's exclusive purpose is creation. Unlike Vishnu and Shiva, he does not contain opposites within himself, and so he never destroys what he has created. According to one tradition he arose out of the "egg of the universe." Originally, he only had one head. He acquired three more when he created woman. After cutting her from his own body he fell in love with her, but she hid herself from him. So that he could always see her from every side, he grew heads to the right, left, and behind. His four heads symbolize his ability to look in all four directions—north, south, east, and west.

VISHNU THE PRESERVER
Vishnu contains and balances good and evil, and all other opposites, within himself. His main task, as preserver, is to maintain the divine order of the universe, keeping the balance between good and evil powers. When evil gets the upper hand, Vishnu comes down to Earth to restore the balance, taking the form of one of the ten incarnations called avatars—beings in whom he lives throughout their lives.

HINDUISM

ONE GOD?
Yes, Brahman who appears in unlimited forms. Each Hindu worships one of these many forms, for example, Brahma, Vishnu, Shiva, Sarasvati, Kali, Lakshmi...

THE AFTERLIFE?
Reincarnation

SCRIPTURES?
Vedas, Upanishads, and others

MAJOR FESTIVALS?
Divali—New year Festival of Lights
Holi—Spring festival
Janmashtami—Birthday of Krishna
Shivaratri—Main festival of Shiva

SACRED ANIMAL?
Cow is the symbol of Earth

Smaller figures represent two of the four Vedas (earliest holy scriptures)

Hinduism is more a way of life than a set of beliefs

SARVEPALLI RADHAKRISHNAN
FORMER PRESIDENT OF INDIA

Shiva's whirling hair holds flowers, snakes, a skull, and a small figure of the goddess Ganga (the sacred Ganges River)

The flaming halo around Shiva symbolizes the cosmos

Shiva beats the [dr]um, he summons a new creation

Shiva's vertical third eye gives light to the world

This hand points to the left foot, beneath which the worshiper can find safe refuge

Left foot is a symbol of liberation

The flame is a symbol of the fire, with which Shiva destroys the universe

SHIVA AS "LORD OF THE DANCE"
Shiva is both destroyer and re-creator. He is depicted in many forms. As Nataraja, Lord of the Dance (the form shown here), he brings the dance or cycle of life to an end in order that a new cycle of life may begin. This statue illustrates a legend in which he subdued 10,000 heretics (nonbelievers) by dancing on the demon of ignorance.

Apasmarapurusa, the black dwarf, demon of ignorance

[S]hiva is adored by two [s]ages (wise men); the one [o]n his right has the lower [b]ody of a snake, the one [o]n his left has tiger legs

Shiva dances in a ring of flames

This sage has the legs of a tiger

[F]lowers, symbols of [p]urity and rebirth, [a]re used to decorate [t]emples and statues

Gods and heroes

THE HINDU SCRIPTURES are full of the adventures of numerous gods and heroes. The *Vedas* tell of Agni the god of fire and sacrifice, Indra the sky-god of war, and Varuna the god of cosmic order. The two great Hindu epics, the *Ramayana* and *Mahabharata*, weave their tales around Rama and Krishna, the most popular of the 10 avatars (incarnations, or forms) of Vishnu. Within the *Mahabharata* is the frequently translated great Indian spiritual classic, *Bhagavad Gita*, the "Song of the Lord". This poem takes the form of a dialogue between the warrior Arjuna and Krishna, acting as his charioteer, as together they fight the war between good and evil symbolized in the battle between the closely related families of the Pandavas and the Kauravas.

Matsya, the fish and first avatar, warned humanity of a great flood

Narasimha, the man-lion and fourth avatar, defeated demons

Kalki, the tenth avatar, is still to come

PRAYING IN THE GANGES
The Ganges River is a sacred river to Hindus, a symbol of life without end. Pilgrims from all over India come to bathe in its holy waters. The city of Varanasi on the Ganges is India's most sacred city and the desired place of death for every Hindu.

Krishna's skin is blue, the color of the oceans and the sky

The flute is a symbol of the cowherders with whom Krishna spent his early years

Krishna is standing on a lotus flower, a symbol of purity and fertility

KRISHNA AVATAR
Many colorful stories are woven around Krishna, eighth avatar of Vishnu. They are told in the great epic, the *Mahabharata*. Vishnu was persuaded to come down to Earth as Krishna when demons were about to overcome the gods. On hearing the news of Krishna's arrival, the demon-king Kansa planned to kill him. But Krishna was fostered by the Yadava chieftain Nanda and his wife, Yashoda, who kept him safe. Countless tales are told of his childish pranks, youthful adventures, and later battles with the demons.

In this ivory image Durga kills the buffalo demon Mahisha

In each of her 10 hands she holds a special weapon; each weapon is a symbol of divine power

THE GODDESS DURGA
Durga (also known as Parvati and Kali) is one of the many forms assumed by Mahadevi Shakti, Shiva's consort. She is the warrior who fights demons, representing the lowest human passions. The worship of Durga often provides the opportunity for some of the greatest Hindu festivals.

his picture, Rama
Sita sit together,
h Rama's faithful
ther Lakshmana
ind them

*Hanuman, the monkey
god, loyal ally of Rama*

RAMA AVATAR

Rama, seventh avatar of Vishnu, is
the embodiment of goodness come
down to Earth. He and his wife Sita
are models of loving husband and
faithful wife. He is respected as the
virtuous god-king who overthrew
the wicked demon Ravana. First, he
and Sita were banished, then Ravana
kidnapped Sita. But Rama defeated
Ravana with the help of
Hanuman, the brave
monkey god, and his
monkey army.

*I am the beginning and
the middle and the end
of all that is. Of all
knowledge I am the
knowledge of the Soul*

KRISHNA IN THE *BHAGAVAD GITA* 10:32

*Ganesha's half halo
indicates his divinity*

*The crown shows
kingly status*

*Noose to
snare
delusion*

*This decorated goad (pointed
stick) represents self-control*

*The large flapping ears
separate the essential
from the nonessential*

*Ganesha writes with a
piece of his broken tusk
after his pen snapped*

*Modaka
sweets*

GANESHA

Ganesha is the firstborn son of
Parvati, who created him out of
divine will while her husband, Shiva,
as away at war. It is told how Shiva,
turning after a long absence to his
heavenly dwelling, saw a stranger
at his door and, enraged at being
denied entrance despite several
warnings, cut off Ganesha's head.
Parvati appeared, only to find that
the victim was her own son.
Desperate to make amends, Shiva
cut off the head of a passing
elephant and placed it on his
son's shoulders. From that day
onward Ganesha has had an
elephant's head. He is the god of
wisdom and the remover of
obstacles. In their prayers,
Hindus ask him to take note
of their requests and convey
them to Shiva.

*Ganesha's great belly
represents space, big enough
to hold all wisdom and life*

Four ways of salvation

HOLY MAN
A sadhu is a wandering holy man. He has no possessions aside from his robes and a few utensils.

WEDDING
Hindu families go to great expe[nse] to provide a wedding ceremor for their children. Marriages a arranged according to caste, kinship, and horoscope. The wedding ceremony contains many highly symbolic elemen and the institution of marriag is highly valued.

Hᴉɴᴅᴜs ᴡɪsʜ ᴛᴏ ᴀᴄʜɪᴇᴠᴇ sᴀʟᴠᴀᴛɪᴏɴ, or *moksha*, by release from the cycle of rebirth. Lightening the load of the karma—the sum of good or bad actions acquired through life—leads toward the final release. There are four basic ways of achieving salvation: the way of action involves performing selfless deeds, in the hope of being blessed for fulfilling duties; the way of knowledge seeks to understand and experience the meaning of life through spiritual research and wisdom. The third is the way of *ashtang* yoga—physical exercises to balance the mind, body, and soul. The way of devotion seeks to be united with the divine through the worship of a particular deity. Traditionally, Hindus are born into one of four castes (social classes), or are "untouchable" outcastes—the lowest rank. Religious duties vary with caste.

Pinnacle represents a mountain, symbolizing upward hopes and ambitions

In the inner sanctum, the worshiper meets the deity

MANDIR
A Hindu temple is called a *mandir*. The building itself represents *Prakriti* (the nature of the universe), and the deity within is the *Purusha* (the Divine Being). On entering a *mandir*, Hindus remove their footwear. This is because a mandir is not only a place of worship but is itself an object of worship. Every part is sacred and holy.

Ornamental windows represent the ears of the divine body

SNAKE DEM[ON]
Snakes play important rol[e] many of the wor[ld's] religions. In the Hi[ndu] religion, *nagas* (sac[red] snakes) have the power to [be] both protective and destruct[ive.] Vishnu is often pictured seated [on] the seven-headed snake, Shes[ha,] which protects him from evil. In [Sri] Lanka, this painted wooden m[ask] of a *naga rassa* (snake demon[)] worn in dances to chase a[way] the evil spirits thought to [be] responsible for sickn[ess.]

Temples are considered to be earthly dwelling places of the gods

26

INCARNATION

The idea that God or the gods make themselves known in bodily form, usually human, is found in many religions. In Hinduism, Vishnu comes down to Earth a number of times in different forms, known as avatars. In Christianity, God takes on human form in Jesus Christ.

The lotus, a symbol of purity, fertility, and creation, is linked with Vishnu

Kamal (lotus-shaped scent shaker) used in domestic worship

ense
older

Main image of Vishnu

Krishna and Balarama

DAILY WORSHIP

Hindus perform *puja* (daily worship) not only in the temple but also in homes. Many families set aside a room for worship; others erect a shrine or image, or display a holy picture, in one corner. This is a portable shrine of Vishnu and shows Vishnu under the protection of Shesha (the snake), with Krishna avatar and his half-brother, Balarama.

INCENSE

Incense is made from a number of woods and resins which, when heated or burned, give off a fragrant smell. The use of incense in divine worship is an ancient and widespread practice. It is associated with sacrifice, honor, purification, and celebration.

*Give me your mind
nd give me your heart,
give me your offerings
and your adoration*

KRISHNA IN THE *BHAGAVAD GITA* 9.34

ARIOT AND CHARIOTEER

e *Bhagavad Gita* consists of a dialogue between
d Krishna and archer Arjuna on a battlefield.
e battle is the war between good and evil,
ion and inaction, knowledge and ignorance,
ief and disbelief. Krishna urges Arjuna
action and promises to be his
arioteer. Vivekananda, a modern
ormer and philosopher,
erpreted their relationship—
e body is the chariot; the
ter senses are the horses;
e mind the reins; and the
ellect the charioteer. So
n crosses the ocean of
ya (illusion). He goes
yond and reaches God.
hen a man is under the
ntrol of his senses, he is
this world. When he
s controlled the senses,
has renounced
e world.

This picture shows a
famous scene from
the *Bhagavad Gita*

The warrior Arjuna

Krishna, acting as Arjuna's charioteer

The Buddhist path

SIDDHARTHA GAUTAMA, THE FOUNDER of Buddhism, lived in the 6th century BCE in northern India. He was brought up to become a king, and married to a beautiful princess who gave him a son. As a young prince, his father protected him from all the sadness of the world outside his palaces. However, while his son was still young, Gautama managed to slip out, and encountered the "Four Sights." First was an old man, second a man sick with disease, and third a corpse being carried to the cremation ground. Finally, he saw a shaven-headed religious beggar, wearing a simple yellow robe, but radiating peace and joy. It was then that Gautama made his "Great Renunciation," leaving his family and life of great comfort to find the answers to this suffering he had seen. For six years he tried and failed, until he went to meditate under a Bodhi tree, where he received his "Great Enlightenment," and became Buddha, which means "the enlightened one."

THE NOBLE EIGHTFOLD PATH
The eight-spoked wheel is a symbol of the Eightfold Path, which is a summary of the Buddha's teaching about how to escape suffering and find enlightenment. The eight paths to follow are: right thought, right understanding, right speech, right action, right livelihood, right effort, right concentration, and right contemplation.

Eyes cast down to show he is meditating; face calm and peaceful

RENUNCIATION
Gautama's decision to leave his family is known as the Great Renunciation. For the next six years, he tried to find release from the weariness of existence. He was reduced to skin and bones, but could not reach this goal. So he left his companions and went to meditate under a Bodhi tree near the Ganges River.

Right hand points down, asking the Earth to witness his enlightenment

The Buddha, meditating in the lotus position (cross-legged posture, feet placed on opposite thighs). In meditation, Buddhists seek to empty their minds of all distracting thoughts and [find] perfect peace.

Halo, one of the marks of Buddhah[ood]

- Siddhartha lived in the 6th century, and had a wealthy family.
- Sat under bodhi tree for 6 days and on the 6th day, recieved his "Great Enlightment"

ENLIGHTENMENT
While meditating under the Bodhi tree, Gautama learned "the Four Noble Truths"—that all life is suffering; that the cause of suffering is desire; that the end of desire means the end of suffering; that desire can be stopped by following the Eightfold Path. The Eightfold Path is also called the Middle Way, because it avoids either living for pleasure or too much self-denial.

BUDDHISM

ONE GOD?
No, but many spiritual beings

THE AFTERLIFE?
Rebirth—we are endlessly reborn in new bodies, unless we achieve "Nirvana"

FOUNDER?
Siddhartha Gautama, the Buddha ("enlightened one"), lived in India c. 560–480 BCE

SCRIPTURES?
The teachings of the Buddha

PRIESTS?
None, but there are spiritual leaders (lamas) and monks

Cultivating enlightenment with the pure mind of meditation… you will completely pass beyond the suffering of this world

GAUTAMA, THE BUDDHA

BUDDHA IMAGES
Here, a Buddhist monk venerates a large image of the Buddha. As Buddhism spread from North India across Asia, the Buddha came to be venerated rather like a god. More and more images of him were made.

Pictures in outer circle teach about karma

The Wheel of Life, or the Everlasting Round

The Lord of Death holds the wheel to symbolize the limits of life

Pictures in inner circle show the six realms (states) of existence

The pig, rooster, and snake represent the poisons of greed, delusion, and hatred, the three ingredients of ignorance that underlie all forms of suffering

The Realm of H... selfishness, i... desire, but... path to en...

Realm of ... ed by igno... thy, and ...

The De... full of ... a Budd... patien...

EEL O...
...ording ...hing, ...y are ...realms of existence. Whi... ...ends on how they behaved in their ...vious life. This is called karma: the law ...which actions are rewarded or punished ...hey deserve, the law of cause and effect in ...ral life. Your karma decides whether your ...t life will be better or worse than this one. ... goal of Gautama's search was to escape ... cycle of rebirth, to find the state of ...piness and peace known as Nirvana.

The Realm of the Gods, happy and proud

The Realm of the Titans, in which envious demigods fight

The Realm of the Hungry Spirits: consumed by greed, they suffer permanent hunger and thirst

In each realm, a Buddha figure appears and helps the beings there

For 6 years Saddhartha searched for peace and freedom but never found it.

• The 4 sights: An old man, a man with a desease, a corpse, and a shaven-headed veleigious beggar, which Saddhartha Saw when he first came out of his palace and saw the world for once.

Devotion and meditation

As buddhism spread outward from India, it developed into two different branches. They are often called "vehicles," since Buddhist *Dharma* (teaching or law) is thought of as a raft or ship carrying people across an ocean of suffering to *Nirvana*—a "Beyond" of salvation and bliss. Theravada, the "Little Vehicle," is mainly found in Southeast Asia. It emphasizes the life of meditation lived by the monk, and its teaching tends toward the view that people are essentially on their own in the universe and can reach Nirvana only by their own efforts. Mahayana, the "Great Vehicle," is the dominant form of Buddhism in Tibet, China, Korea, Vietnam, and Japan. Mahayana Buddhists believe that people are not alone and must help one another. They can also receive help from the Buddha, and other buddhas, and from bodhisattvas (almost-buddhas who have paused before Nirvana to help others). Salvation is available to all through faith and devotion.

PLACES OF WORSHIP
After the Buddha's death, his body was cremated and his ashes distributed among his followers. They formed the original relics (holy objects) and were housed and worshiped in stupas (great sacred mounds). In parts of Asia, stupas are called pagodas. Later, temples were built, where worship was offered in the presence of images of the Buddha and bodhisattvas.

Monks in the precincts of the Wat Po temple in Thailand

PLACES OF MEDITATION
Buddhism gave rise to numerous sects and practices within and outside the two main vehicles. One is Zen, which originated in Chinese ways of meditation. Zen is widespread in Japan and there are Zen gardens across the country. Zen meditation has strict rules. The most important are to sit in the lotus position and to address riddles that have no answer (these help in breaking free from the mind). For example, "When you clap hands, you hear a sound. Now listen to one hand clapping."

FOCUS OF DEVOTION
Originally, the Buddha was a famous and greatly honored human being devoted to working out his own salvation and teaching others. In Mahayana Buddhism, he came to be revered as a supernatural being. His image sits in temples. Beside it there may be other buddhas, and bodhisattvas such as Avalokiteshvara, the embodiment of compassion, and Akakasagarbha, the bodhisattva of infinite happiness.

Bodhisattva Avalokiteshvara (which means "The lord who looks down")

Buddha Amoghasiddhi, one of the five "meditation buddhas"

Dipankara Buddha, the "causer of light"

Seven other bodhisattvas

Worn around hips

Worn over shoulder

Worn on top for ceremonial occasions or for traveling

Belt or girdle

Razor

Needle and thread

Sharpening stone

Water Strainer

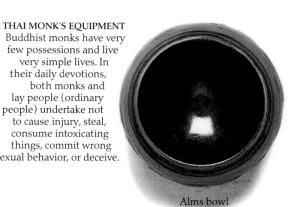

THAI MONK'S EQUIPMENT
Buddhist monks have very few possessions and live very simple lives. In their daily devotions, both monks and lay people (ordinary people) undertake not to cause injury, steal, consume intoxicating things, commit wrong sexual behavior, or deceive.

Alms bowl

To the Buddha for refuge I go
To the Dharma for refuge I go
To the Sangha for refuge I go

GAUTAMA, THE BUDDHA

Lid from alms bowl used as plate

REINCARNATION

he belief that we live many different lives on Earth. When we die, we spend time in a disembodied state before being reborn in a different bodily form. What we are reborn as depends on our previous behavior this is the law of karma). Buddhist and Hindu forms f this belief differ. Buddhists prefer the word rebirth.

NK IN MEDITATION
r his enlightenment, the Buddha ed a community of monks. Ever e, the Sangha, the community onks, has been central to dhism. Even today, in Buddhist land, it is customary for most ng men to enter a monastery, ly for a month. Meditation so very important. In itation, Buddhists attempt ill the mind and its endless of thoughts, ideas, and es, replacing them with te of inner stillness. In this ess, it is said, meditators me aware of their amental state and gain, me, enlightenment.

Hands in meditative position

Mat for meditation

Legs crossed in half-lotus position

Tibetan Buddhism

BUDDHISM CAME TO TIBET from India in the 8th century. By that time, Indian Buddhism had adapted a complicated set of rituals and "magic" from folk religion to help people to find their way to Nirvana. This branch of Buddhism was written in sacred, secret books called tantras, so it was called Tantrism. It included the use of mystic diagrams called mandalas, and sacred phrases or sayings called mantras, which disciples said over and over again. The religion that came to dominate Tibet was a mixture of Tantric and other Mahayana teachings. In Tibet, it was developed further by spiritual leaders called lamas, who are usually monks. Lamas belong to a number of different groups, or schools. These schools are based around various powerful monasteries: their ideas and practices vary, but they have usually existed in harmony. One of a lama's tasks is to guide a dying person's spirit in the time between death and rebirth. Lamas spend many years learning and meditating to gain this wisdom.

TIBET AND BEYOND
In modern times, Tibetan Buddhism has had an increasing influence abroad. Tibetans and Buddhists of different traditions, such as these monks in Shanghai, are happy to share their experience and wisdom.

Vairochana, foremost of the Meditation Buddhas, perfects knowledge

Ratnasambhava, "The Beautifier," perfects goodness and beauty

Amitabha, "Infinite Compassion," perfects speech

Vajrasattva, "The Unchanging," perfects wisdom

Amoghasiddhi, "Almight[y] Conqueror," perfects actio[n]

THE FIVE BUDDHAS
This Tibetan lama's ritual headdress displays the "Buddhas of Meditation." According to *The Tibetan Book of the Dead*, these Buddhas dwell in the heavenly worlds. Each personifies an aspect of "Divine Being," the ultimate reality or wisdom. They meet a dead person's spirit, and the spirit's reaction shows how enlightened the person is and decides how the person will be reborn.

The demon has glaring eyes, protruding tusks, and a jutting tongue

RITUAL PROTECTION
In Indian mythology, the god Shiva creates a demon who will be the supreme destructive force of the universe. The grotesque face of this demon, called "the face of glory," is often placed on temples of Shiva as a protective device. This ritual amulet is a Tibetan adaptation of the Indian symbol and is worn to terrify demons and protect the wearer.

...NERATING RELICS

...n soon after the Buddha's death, ...dhists began to collect the ...sical remains and belongings ...oly persons and to venerate ...m as relics (holy objects). Here, ...ressions of shrines and Buddha ...ges have been molded from ...a ashes. After the cremation of ...ma, ashes are collected, mixed ...h clay, molded into tablets, ...placed in cases or shrines.

Bodhisattvas have graceful bodies, wear long robes and jewelry, and hold religious implements

BODHISATTVA OF COMPASSION
The story is told of how Avalokiteshvara, the Bodhisattva of Compassion, vowed to save all ...onscious beings, but soon became so overwhelmed ...by the task that his head split into a thousand pieces. ...he pieces were put back together again to form eleven ...eads, looking in all directions. With these heads and ...a thousand arms, nowhere is out of reach of ...his love and mercy. In China, he is Kuan Yin, ...and in Japan Kwannon, Goddess of Love and ...Mercy. In Tibet today, he becomes reincarnate ...n the person of the Dalai Lama, now in exile ...but still the leading lama.

...UNG LAMAS
...etan Buddhism has had a strong ...ritual and moral influence on ...etans. Since the Communist ...eover of 1950, the influence of ...gion has weakened. Many do still ...ctice their devotions, however, and ...rong movement continues among ...ugees. Here, young lamas blow ...rns as part of a monastic ritual.

PRAYER WHEEL
A prayer wheel contains a mantra, a prayer or chant that is repeated many times. Each turn of the wheel counts as a prayer said and merit gained. The mantra in this prayer wheel is usually translated as "Hail to the jewel in the lotus" and is directed to Avalokiteshvara.

Chain helps wheel to spin

Mantra fits inside prayer wheel

He holds objects that illustrate Buddhist truths

As the wheel is spun, the heavy head spins fast

This Avalokiteshvara stands on a lotus-flower throne that rises on a stalk out of swirling waters

When the breath has ceased... the Knower will be experiencing the Clear Light of the natural condition

THE TIBETAN BOOK OF THE DEAD, 1.1

This gilt bronze statue was made in the 18th century

The Tao principle

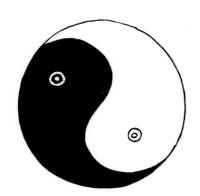

YIN AND YANG
The Yin-Yang symbol represents the two halves of the Tao, the two opposite, complementary principles Taoists see in nature: Yin—dark, female, passive, soft; and Yang—light, male, active, hard.

Taoists believe that there is a principle, or force, running through the whole of the natural world, and controlling it. They call this principle the Tao. Tao means way, or path. To follow the Tao is to follow the way of nature. It is sometimes called the "watercourse way" because Taoists see water as a picture of the Tao at work. Water is soft and yielding, it flows effortlessly to humble places, yet it is also the most powerful of substances, and it nourishes all life. There are two kinds of Taoism—the popular and the philosophical. The followers of philosophical Taoism are likely to be mystical and peaceful. By stilling the inner self, their senses, and appetites, they gain an understanding of the Tao, and try to live in oneness and harmony with it. The focus of popular Taoism is different. It includes very many gods, goddesses, and spiritual beings, whose help believers seek, and demons, who are feared. Its followers use magic and ritual to harness *Te*—virtue or power—in the hope of becoming immortal.

Li Ti'eh-kuai used to go in spirit to visit Lao-tzu in the celestial regions; he once stayed so long that his body had gone when he came back, so his spirit had to enter the body of a lame beggar

Lu Tung-pin overcame a series of temptations and was given a magic sword, with which he killed dragons and fought evil

Ho Hsien-ku lived on powdered mother-of-pearl and moonbeams; her emblem is the lotus

THE FOUNDER
According to Taoist tradition, Lao-tzu lived in central China in the 6th century BCE, at the same time as Confucius, who is said to have visited him as a young man. Lao-tzu worked as keeper of archives for the Chou dynasty. In later life, tired of Chou corruption, he tried to flee to Tibet. But he was stopped at the border and refused permission to leave unless he left behind a record of his teachings. In 3 days, he produced the *Tao Te Ching*, the greatest of Taoist writings. Then he handed it over and rode away on a water buffalo, never to be heard of again.

Ts'ao Kuo-chiu, patron of the theater, wears a court headdress and official robes, and holds his emblem in one hand

THE EIGHT IMMORTALS
The Eight Immortals are legendary beings believed to have attained immortality, through their practice of the Tao principle. They are said to have lived on Earth at various times, and each represents a different condition in life—poverty, wealth, aristocracy, low social status, age, youth, masculinity, and femininity. Here they are shown with a fabulous being named Si Wang Mu, who has the power to give away the peaches of immortality, which grow on the peach tree of the genii, beside the Lake of Gems in the West.

THE FAIRY CRANE
The traditional Chinese focus on death, immortality, and the ancestors means that funerals—and the rituals surrounding them—are often very important. A paper fairy crane is often carried at the head of the funeral procession of priests (shown here, with the abbot in his chair). The crane symbolizes a winged messenger from heaven, and when the paper crane is burned, it is believed that the departed soul rides to heaven on the winged messenger's back.

Chang Kuo-lao, a magician, could make himself invisible

> *To exist means to embrace the Yang principle (of the light) and turn one's back on the Yin (of the dark)*

TAO TE CHING

The magical being Si Wang Mu, here shown as male, more often appears as female

Han Hsiang-tzu is patron of musicians; his emblem is the flute

Lan Ts'ai-ho, patron of florists, holds aloft her emblem, the flower-basket

Chung-li Ch'uan holds a fan with which he revives the souls of the dead

GOD OF LONGEVITY
Chinese people see long life as a very desirable blessing. Therefore Shou-lai, god of longevity, is a popular deity. He is often depicted, either alone or with the Eight Immortals. His image may be carved in wood and stone, cast in bronze and porcelain, or used as a motif in embroidery and porcelain-painting. He is easily identified by his high, bulging forehead and bald head.

RITUAL POWER
Popular Taoism provides for everyday religious needs. Whatever the official philosophy, belief in personal gods and personalized spirits persists, and people still seek their help. Here priests burn incense at a popular ceremony where power (*Te*) is harnessed through magic and ritual. Priests are mainly concerned with cures for sickness and disease and with the casting out of evil spirits.

Confucian piety

FOR MANY, CONFUCIANISM is a way of life, a code of behavior, rather than a religion. Confucians may combine following their master, Confucius, with belief in any god or none. Confucius stressed the importance of *li*, which means proper or orderly conduct. He taught his followers to be "gentlemen." A gentleman is always courteous, fair, respectful to his superiors, and kind to ordinary people. He also practices "filial piety"—his duty to respect and care for his parents. Because of his belief in filial piety, Confucius supported the ancient practice of venerating (giving great respect and honor to) ancestors. He wished to bring order and harmony to society, with everyone doing their duty. He taught that worshiping God and the spirits and honoring one's ancestors means nothing unless the service of other people comes first.

CONFUCIUS
Confucius, or K'ung Fu-tzu, (551–479 BCE) was China's first great philosopher. His name means "Master King"; a legend says that when he was born it was foretold that he would be "a king without a crown." His discussions and sayings are collected together in *The Analects*.

THE THREE WAYS
China is the land of the "Three Ways," Confucianism, Taoism, and Buddhism. For more than 2,000 years, they have all played a major role in Chinese life and thought. Confucianism emphasized order and respect, Taoism provided a mystical understanding of the world, and Buddhism offered salvation through compassion and devotion. As they developed, they merged with each other, and with the age-old folk religion of China, centered on home and family. This painting symbolically shows how the Three Ways mix by representing their three founders together: Buddha (left), Confucius (center), and Lao-tzu (right).

CONFUCIUS DAY CEREMONY
Confucius did not try to found a religion, but to teach a way of life based on rules of good behavior. However, after his death, shrines were built in his honor, and Confucianism became the state religion of China.

Modern Confucian temple at Taipei in Taiwan

Priests honor Confucius Day

Bell was hung on a loop so it could vibrate clearly

MUSIC FOR THE MIND

The Chinese people believed that the music of bells calmed the mind and helped clear thinking. It is said that when he heard a piece of ritual bell music, Confucius was inspired to give up worldly comforts and live on rice and water for three months.

What you do not want done to yourself, do not do to others

Large bronze bell struck like a gong from the outside

Guardian figures often have the look of ferocious animals so they are more effective in frightening away harmful spirits

GUARDIAN FIGURES

On the ridge tiles and at the corners of the roofs of important Chinese buildings, under their eaves and outside tombs, stand figures representing guardian spirits who ward off evil. It is an ancient custom. This guardian figure comes from a tomb of the Tang dynasty, which ruled China from 618 to 907.

Ornate and colorful figures are found in buildings and tombs

...th and death dates and ...ails of ancestors are ...cribed on tablet

ANCESTOR TABLETS

According to Chinese folk religion, ancestors live on in the form of spirits, to whom sacrifices are offered. When a relative is buried, a small stone tablet is taken to the grave. It is then carried back to the house and placed in a shrine.

A man honors his ancestors and places offerings before their tablet so that they will protect and honor him.

TOMB STORE

Objects such as this model storehouse were placed in tombs to provide for the dead person's needs in the afterlife. Descendants went to the tomb once a year to perform a ceremony of ancestor veneration at the entrance.

Shinto harmony

Sʜɪɴᴛᴏ ɪs ᴛʜᴇ ᴍᴏsᴛ ᴀɴᴄɪᴇɴᴛ religion of Japan. The name means "the way of the gods." It is a religion of nature, focused on kami, which are supernatural spirits, or gods, in which the force of nature is concentrated. They include seas and mountains; animals, birds, and plants; even ancestors have the powers of kami. It is said there are eight million kami, worshiped at national, local, and household shrines all over Japan. The force of nature itself is also called kami, and is seen as divine. It inspires a feeling of awe and wonder. The most important shrines are associated with places of natural beauty—on the mountains, in the forests, and near the sea.

SACRED GATE
Since ancient times, Shinto shrines have been marked by entrance gates called *torii*. Because a beautiful natural setting, such as a sacred open space among trees or rocks, was often sufficient as a shrine, torii stood in such places. The great red torii to the famous island shrine of Itsukushima stands in the waters of the Inland Sea and is one of the great sights of Japan.

SHINTO GODDESS
Kami are rarely represented in the form of images to be worshiped. One exception is Nakatsu-hime, goddess of the Eight-Island Country directly below heaven. In one cult she is seen as an incarnation of the Buddhist goddess Kannon.

The god named Hand Strength Male approaching the cave to bring out the Sun goddess

The gods decked out the tree of heaven with jewels and a mirror, then made music and danced to attract Amaterasu's attention

THE SUN GODDESS AMATERASU
Amaterasu Omikami, the Sun goddess, is the supreme Shinto god. Her shrine at Ise is the most popular in Japan. One myth tells that her brother, the Storm god, made her so angry that she hid in a cave, bringing darkness to the Earth. To persuade her to come out, the other gods hung jewels and a mirror on the tree of heaven and danced for her. She looked out to see what was happening, saw herself in the mirror and, while watching, fascinated, was pulled outside. Since then, dawn has always followed night.

MOUNT FUJI
Since ancient times, mountains have been seen as special dwelling places of the gods. Much Shinto art deals with sacred mountains, figures, cults, shrines, settings, or themes. Shinto art also reflects the long interaction between Shinto and Buddhism.

HOLINESS

What is "holy" is separate and different, something "other"—far beyond the ordinary. Either beings or places may be holy or sacred. When we experience the holy, we feel awe and wonder, or blessing, or dread, or peace, or a sense of "wholeness." The word "holiness" also refers to moral or spiritual goodness.

Festivals are important in Shinto practice as the time when a shrine's worshipers focus on it. One of the greatest is the Gion Festival, held annually since the 16th century. Local people decorate and wheel tall floats through the streets of Kyoto. During one such festival, this young boy pays his respects to his local god.

Mallet to grant wishes

Boy taking part in the Gion festival

NTO AND
DHISM

nto is more a
gion of experience
n of doctrine (set beliefs), so
asily blended with Buddhism
r Buddhism reached Japan in
6th century CE. The kami were
n seen as local manifestations
uddhas and boddhisattvas,
Buddhist temples existed
ide, or inside, Shinto shrines.
dhist monks such as those
ve still take part in the great
nto festivals.

*Wherever the "energy"
of the universe attains
a particular intensity,
revealing itself as
beauty, power, wonder,
here the ultimate becomes
apparent: there is "kami"*

FOSCO MARAINI IN *JAPAN: PATTERNS OF CONTINUITY*

The god Daikoku, one of the seven gods of fortune

The god's rat attendant

Sack of rice

E SEVEN GODS
e seven gods of fortune, or good luck,
re originally Buddhist deities and are
w worshiped in Shinto, too—another
mple of how Buddhism and Shinto mix.
ikoku is the god of wealth and patron of
mers. He is often pictured with his son,
isu, god of honest labor. He is usually shown
ing on sacks of rice, with a bag of jewels on
shoulder, a golden Sun disk on his chest,
d a mallet with which he grants wishes. His
endant is a rat, sometimes shown nibbling
ay at the rice sacks. Daikoku is rich though,
d always good humored about it. He is also
d to be fond of children.

Jain respect for life

THE BIRTH OF MAHAVIRA
Vardhamana Mahavira was the 24th and last Tirthankara. Born around 540 BCE, he was brought up as a prince, but at the age of 28 he gave up everything to seek liberation from the endless round of birth-death-rebirth. He became a beggar and an ascetic (a person who lives a life of self-denial). At about the age of 40, he achieved full enlightenment. He devoted the rest of his life to spreading his beliefs and organizing a community of followers.

JAINISM IS AN ANCIENT INDIAN RELIGION. Its most distinctive doctrine is its belief in *ahimsa*, or nonviolence to living things, which has influenced many nonJains, including Mahatma Gandhi. Jains believe that the universe has neither beginning nor end—there is no creator god. The universe passes through a never-ending number of cosmic cycles. Each cycle is divided into periods of ascent and descent, during which civilization rises then falls. Tirthankaras (ford-makers) appear; there are 24 in each cycle. They first of all conquer their own passions and emotions, thus liberating and perfecting themselves, and then guide others across the "river of transmigration" (the journey of the soul from one life to the next). Jains believe that the final Tirthankara of the present period was Mahavira, founder of Jainism. Tirthankaras are also called Jinas (conquerors)—the word from which Jains take their name.

Right knowledge comes through keeping the Jain creed, right faith through believing it, and right conduct through following it

THE "THREE JEWELS"

TOTAL DETACHMENT
The inner shrine of a Jain temple is dominated by a principal image of the Tirthankara to whom the temple is dedicated. It is usually flanked by two attendants and surrounded by smaller images of the remaining 23 Tirthankaras. Here, the 20th Tirthankara sits in passionless detachment for Jains to contemplate.

These diamond- or pear-shaped marks are often shown on Tirthankaras and are good omens

Each Tirthankara has a symbol, in this case the tortoise

PARSHVA
Parshva, the 23rd Tirthankara, was a famous teacher who lived in and around Varanasi, India, about 850 BCE. Here, he is shown flanked on either side by his two attendants, and surrounded by other Tirthankaras. Above his head is a canopy formed by the seven-headed cobra Ananta, "the endless," who guards him.

Pilgrims bathing the 60-ft- (18-m-) high stone image of the hero Gomateshvara with turmeric

...TIVALS
...tivals play an important part in Jain life. They ...y be solemn like Pajjusana, which closes the ...n year, or joyful like Divali, the great Hindu ...tival that has been adapted in honor of ...havira's liberation and enlightenment.

DEITIES IN JAINISM

Jains do not worship gods; they contemplate Tirthankaras. That is the theory. In practice, however, many ordinary Jains pray to Hindu deities, and many Jain temples contain images of minor Hindu gods and goddesses. Among the most popular is Sarasvati, goddess of wisdom and the arts.

Sarasvati holds symbolic objects in her hands; the prayer beads in her upper left hand show her piety

The five seated figures around Sarasvati are Tirthankaras

As goddess of wisdom and writing, she holds a palm-leaf manuscript (now broken)

Two fly-whisk holders fan Sarasvati

Two donors are shown kneeling before the goddess

...NUNCIATION
...e Jain monk is a homeless wanderer. ... owns hardly anything except his ...es, pieces of cloth with which to strain ...ects away when he drinks, and a brush ...h which to sweep insects from the ...h before him, so as not to hurt them.

NONVIOLENCE

Nonviolence, or *ahimsa*, is the principle of not inflicting harm on others, particularly human beings. For some, particularly Jains, the idea is extended to any living thing. Nonviolence starts with an attitude of mind. It is against harmful thoughts as well as aggressive deeds.

Sikh teaching

THE SIKH STANDARD
The Sikh emblem, the *nishan sahib*, contains a ring of steel representing the unity of God, a two-edged sword symbolizing God's concern for truth and justice, and two crossed, curved swords around the outside to signify God's spiritual power. A flag with the *nishan sahib* on it is flown from every gurdwara (Sikh temple).

Sᴵᴋʜs ᴄᴀɴ ʙᴇ ꜰᴏᴜɴᴅ in almost every part of the world. Their gurdwaras (temples) adorn the cities of Britain, East Africa, Malaysia, the west coast of Canada, and the United States. The vast majority, however, live in India. Their founder, Guru Nanak, was born in the Punjab in 1469. Nanak taught a new doctrine of salvation, centering on two basic ideas, one about the nature of God, one about the nature of humankind. To Sikhs, God is single and personal. He is the Creator with whom the individual must develop the most intimate of relationships. People are willfully blind; they shut their eyes to this divine revelation and need a guru (a spiritual guide) to teach them. The idea of the guru lies at the heart of the Sikh religion—even the name "Sikh" comes from an old word meaning "disciple." Sikhs recognize 12 gurus—God; Nanak and nine other human gurus, and the 12th guru, *Guru Granth Sahib*, the Sikh holy book.

THE GOLDEN TEMPLE
The Golden Temple at Amritsar is the central shrine of Sikhism, and its most important place of pilgrimage. On entering, pilgrims offer coins and each receives a small portion of *karah parshad* (holy food that symbolizes equality and brotherhood). They then sit and listen to the singing of passages from the scriptures. The water surrounding the temple is considered especially holy and pilgrims often bathe in it.

Silk cloth placed over cover of holy book

FOCUS OF WORSHIP
Gurdwara literally means "the door of the guru" and the temple houses the holy scriptures, called the *Guru Granth Sahib*. The scriptures contain spiritual poetry written by the 10 human gurus. The *Granth* is the supreme authority for Sikhs and Sikh worship centers on its guidance. The book is greatly revered; it is placed on a cushion under a canopy and covered with a silk cloth in the main body of the temple.

Even when the pages of the Granth are being read, its cover is covered with silk cloths (not shown here)

Guru Nanak, founder
of the Sikh religion

The other nine human
gurus (shown with haloes)
sit around Guru Nanak

THE 12 GURUS

[Sikh]ism is sometimes called [Guru]mat, meaning "the Guru's [doc]trine." God, the original Guru, [imp]arted his message to his chosen [disc]iple, Nanak, first of a series of 10 [hum]an gurus. Gurus were chosen by [thei]r predecessors for their spiritual [insi]ght. Gobind Singh (1666–1708) [was] the last. He transferred his [aut]hority to the community and the [scri]ptures. He said that the scriptures [wou]ld be their guru, so the holy [boo]k, called the *Guru Granth Sahib*, [is th]e 12th guru.

God is One, He is the True Name, He is the Creator

THE OPENING WORDS OF THE *GURU GRANTH SAHIB*

The *kara*
(steel bangle)

The *kangha*
(comb)

THE FIVE K'S

The Khalsa (community) was founded by Gobind Singh, last of the 10 human gurus. Young Sikhs enter at puberty. It has five outward symbols, known as the "five Ks": the sword, comb, bangle, uncut hair (with a turban worn over it), and breeches.

The *kirpan*
(sword)

The language is a mixture of Punjabi, Persian, Sanskrit, and Khariboli and is sung to classical Indian chants; most of the book is poetry

SIGN OF RESPECT

The *chauri*, or whisk, is a symbol of authority and is waved over the holy book to show honor and respect for it, because a whisk would once have been waved over a human guru in the Punjab (to keep the flies away), and the book is now the guru. The *chauri* can be made of peacock feathers, yak hair, goat hair, or, as here, synthetic material.

THE GURU GRANTH SAHIB

The *Guru Granth Sahib* is a collection of the teachings of Guru Nanak and the other human gurus. At the beginning are a number of verses attributed to Nanak himself, and these are recited by Sikhs in their morning prayers. Next come poems and hymns that are attributed to various gurus and always sung. Central to the scriptures is the idea of salvation. A Sikh is awakened by the divine guru and, through meditation on the divine Name and hearing the divine Word, the disciple ultimately unites with the divine harmony.

Zoroastrianism

On the extreme edge of the western Iranian desert, in and around Mumbai in India, in East Africa, and in many of the major cities of the world are pockets of a small community totaling no more than 130,000 members worldwide. They are the Zoroastrians, known in India as the Parsis or "Persians," followers of the prophet Zoroaster, who lived in ancient Persia. Zoroaster called for people to live the "good life" and follow Ahura Mazda, the "Supreme Creator," or "Wise Lord," symbolized by fire. Zoroaster believed that the world was essentially good, though tainted by evil. He also believed that, just as Ahura Mazda is responsible for all the good in life, so misery and suffering are the work of an independent force of evil, Angra Mainyu. The two powers are locked in conflict. It is the duty of all people to support the good. Those who choose good are rewarded with happiness. Those who choose evil end in sorrow. Zoroaster taught that in the end, good would triumph over evil.

GUARDIAN SPIRIT
Zoroastrians see this image as a fravashi, a guardian spirit. They say that everyone is watched over by a fravashi. Fravashis represent the good, or the God-essence, in people. They help those who ask them and work for good in the universe. This symbol can also be seen as representing "the spiritual self," or Ahura Mazda. It is found very often in Zoroastrianism.

THE AGE OF RESPONSIBILITY
Before puberty, between the ages of seven and 12, young Zoroastrians are initiated into their faith in the Navjote ceremony, at which they symbolically take on the responsibility to uphold the ideas and morals of Zoroastrianism. They are given a sacred thread, or *kushti*, to wear, and a sacred vest, or *sudreh*. The vest is white, for purity and renewal. The 72 strands of the thread symbolize a universal fellowship.

THANKSGIVING CEREMONY
A Jashan is a ceremony of thanksgiving performed by two or more priests. The officiating priest is known as the zaotar and his assistant as the raspi. Jashan ensures the well-being of both physical and spiritual worlds as the living offer thanks and ask for blessings from the spiritual world. All seven "Bounteous Immortals" (Amesha Spentas), coworkers with Ahura Mazda, and departed virtuous souls are ritually invited down to join the Jashan. The Bounteous Immortals are the guardians of the seven good creations—the sky, waters, Earth, plants, cattle, humans, and fire—represented symbolically by the materials and implements used.

DRINK OF IMMORTALITY
The ritual most associated with Zoroastrians is that of tending the sacred fire. In Yasna, a major prayer ceremony, the sacred liquor haoma (made of the juice of a plant) is offered to the sacred fire. The offering and drinking of this consecrated juice confers immortality on the worshiper.

Mask over face because sacred objec[t] would be contaminated if sneezed on

Milk represents cattle, the fifth creation

Wine represents hospitality

Fruits and flowers represent plants, the fourth creation

Water represents t[he] second creati[on]

Flowerbu[ds] represent t[he] Bounteo[us] Immort[als]

All the metallic implements represent the sky, the first creation

Zoroaster or, more correctly, Zarathusthra in ancient Persian, is commonly believed to have lived between 1500 and [.]0 BCE, which would make him the earliest known f the great prophets of the world's religions. Little is known about his life, except that he was a priest as well as a ophet, and was married ith several children. The ligion he founded was for more than 1,000 years he official religion of Persia (now Iran), ne of the world's greatest empires.

rganyu (fire-e); sandalwood ns continuously t to represent l, the source of t and life

The traditional oil lamp which is kept burning

FIRE TEMPLE

Originally, Zoroastrian worship was conducted in the open air. Today, however, every Zoroastrian community worships in a fire temple where prayer rituals are performed in the presence of a sacred fire, which is seen as a living embodiment of Ahura Mazda. No images are allowed, and only Zoroastrians may enter the temple. Before entering, worshipers wash their hands and faces and then perform the *kushti* prayer ritual. Then they slip off their shoes to enter the fire temple to present themselves before the fire. They apply a pinch of ash from the sacred fire to their foreheads, then pray, focusing on the pure light of Ahura Mazda.

Good thoughts, good words, good deeds

THE ZOROASTRIAN IDEAL

Tray of sandalwood and frankincense

Flat circular spoon used by the raspi (assistant priest) to offer sandalwood and frankincense to the fire

The Jewish nation

CROSSING THE RED SEA
According to the Bible, the descendants of Jacob's 12 sons, the 12 tribes of Israel, became slaves in Egypt. Eventually, God called Moses to lead them out of slavery. God had to send ten plagues on Egypt before Pharaoh would let them go. Even then, Pharaoh changed his mind and sent his army to trap them by the Red Sea. God parted the sea for the Israelites. When the Egyptians tried to cross, the sea closed over them. This is one of the events celebrated at the annual Passover festival. In such festivals, the history of the Jewish people is kept alive, and the lessons it has taught them about God are remembered.

THE JEWISH PEOPLE trace their ancestry back to three ancient leaders known as the patriarchs—Abraham, his son Isaac, and his grandson Jacob. In their daily prayers, Jews still call themselves "children of Abraham." They call their nation Israel because God renamed Jacob, and called him Israel. Their story began when Abraham left what is now Iraq in about 1800 BCE to settle in Canaan, the "Promised Land," now known as Palestine or Israel. Later, Jacob's sons went to Egypt. Around 1250 BCE, their descendants, the Hebrews, were led out by Moses, in the journey known as the Exodus. On the way the God of the patriarchs appeared to Moses on Mount Sinai and made a covenant (agreement) with Israel. It was enshrined in the Ten Commandments, and later in the rest of the Torah, the "law of Moses." Ever since, this God-given religious law has been at the heart of Israel's identity as a people. Jews see God as both the God of Israel, his "chosen people," and also the creator and ruler of all that is, the God who controls history, all-powerful and all-loving.

THE WESTERN WALL
The Western Wall is all that remains of the second Temple, built by King Herod, that stood in Jerusalem 2,000 years ago, when Jerusalem was the capital of the ancient Jewish kingdom. The Temple was the center of Jewish worship until it was destroyed by the Romans in 70 CE, after which the Jews were scattered and did not have their own state for 1,900 years. The wall is a symbol of the Temple and a memorial of its destruction. It is the holiest site for Jews in Jerusalem.

The wall used to be called the Wailing Wall because it was associated with crying for the destruction of the Temple

Jewish people come from all over the world to pray at the wall

A BABY BOY
When God made a covenant with Abraham, he commanded that all boys born into Abraham's people should be circumcised as a sign of God's choice of Israel as his chosen people. They are circumcised still, eight days after birth. This is a cloth made for a baby boy.

The Hebrew reads "May he live for the Torah, the Huppah, and good deeds"

The Huppah, or Wedding Canopy—the indispensable covering for the bridal pair during the marriage ceremony

The Torah scroll

שְׁמַע יִשְׂרָאֵל יְהוָה אֱלֹהֵינוּ יְהוָה אֶחָד וְאָהַבְתָּ אֵת יְהוָה אֱלֹהֶיךָ בְּכָל לְבָבְךָ וּבְכָל
נַפְשְׁךָ וּבְכָל מְאֹדֶךָ וְהָיוּ הַדְּבָרִים הָאֵלֶּה אֲשֶׁר אָנֹכִי מְצַוְּךָ הַיּוֹם עַל לְבָבֶךָ וְשִׁנַּנְתָּם
לְבָנֶיךָ וְדִבַּרְתָּ בָּם בְּשִׁבְתְּךָ בְּבֵיתֶךָ וּבְלֶכְתְּךָ בַדֶּרֶךְ וּבְשָׁכְבְּךָ וּבְקוּמֶךָ וּקְשַׁרְתָּם
לְאוֹת עַל יָדֶךָ וְהָיוּ לְטֹטָפֹת בֵּין עֵינֶיךָ וּכְתַבְתָּם עַל מְזֻזוֹת בֵּיתֶךָ וּבִשְׁעָרֶיךָ

The first part of the biblical text of the Shema

A ninth candle, called the servant candle, is used to light the rest

The star of David, Israel's greatest king

THE MEZUZAH
The Mezuzah is a tiny parchment scroll inscribed with biblical texts and enclosed in a case. Traditionally, Mezuzahs are attached to the door frames of Jewish homes. They usually contain the words of the Shema from the Bible, which calls God's people to love him totally. Religious Jews repeat the Shema morning and evening because it sums up the heart of their faith.

A candle is lit for each of the eight days of the festival

r, O Israel: the Lord your
d, the Lord is one… Love
e Lord your God with all
r heart, and with all your
, and with all your might

THE BEGINNING OF THE SHEMA

HANUKKAH, FESTIVAL OF LIGHTS
Hanukkah is an eight-day midwinter festival marked by the lighting of ritual candles. It celebrates the rededication of the temple of Jerusalem by Judas Maccabeus after he had recaptured it from an enemy army in 164 BCE. The Jewish religious year includes a number of festivals, which remind Jews of God's faithfulness to his people in the past and help them to be dedicated to him.

JUDAISM
ONE GOD?
Yes
THE AFTERLIFE?
Yes, but Judaism is mainly concerned with this life
FOUNDERS?
Abraham, father of the Jewish people, lived in the Middle East c. 1800 BCE Moses, gave the Torah (the law), lived in the Middle East c. 1250 BCE
SCRIPTURES?
The Jewish Bible, of which the Torah (the law of Moses) is the most important part
A WRITTEN CODE?
The Torah, which gives guidance for all aspects of life

People of the Torah

THE ARK
In a synagogue (Jewish meeting place), the ark holds the scrolls of the Torah. It sits behind a curtain in the synagogue wall that faces toward Jerusalem. The original Ark of the Covenant held the Ten Commandments while Israel journeyed from Egypt toward the Promised Land.

Bar Mitzvah ceremony

AT THE HEART of the Jewish religion is the Torah, "the Law," written in the first five books of the Hebrew Bible. Torah does not only mean "law," but also "teaching" and "guidance." In the Torah, God has given teaching about himself, his purposes, and how he wishes his people to obey him in every part of their lives. For a religious Jew, to obey the Torah is to follow God's guidance. The reading of the Torah is a major part of worship in the synagogue (assembly). People also respond to God by communicating with him in prayer. Jewish people have a special role in God's plans for humanity, since it was to them that God revealed the Torah. They look forward to a time when God will send his Messiah ("anointed one") to announce the final setting up of God's rule, or kingdom, on Earth.

COMING OF AGE
When a Jewish boy reaches 13, he becomes Bar Mitzvah, "a son of the commandment." He is then considered to be a responsible adult, and is expected to follow all the commandments of the Law. For a girl, the age of responsibility is 12.

The Hebrew text reads "Crown of the Torah"

The crown is a symbol of the Torah because the Torah is seen as the crowning glory of Jewish life

The lion is a common Jewish symbol, originally associated with the tribe of Judah, one of the 12 tribes of Israel

TORAH AND MANTLE
The Western tradition is for Torah scrolls to be kept covered by an embroidered mantle (left). In the Eastern tradition of North Africa and the Middle East, they are kept in a rigid container.

The deeper you dig into the Torah, the more treasures you uncover

ISAAC BASHEVIS SINGER

SIGN OF RESPECT

A strictly religious Jewish man prays three times a day—in the morning, afternoon, and evening—either at home or in the synagogue. When he prays, he covers his head with a hat, or a skull-cap, known as *yarmulka* or *kippah*. When he goes out, an orthodox Jew may continue to cover his head as a sign of respect for God.

WEARING THE TORAH

During their daily prayers, Jewish men wear a pair of small black leather boxes containing passages from the Torah strapped to their upper left arms and above their foreheads. These boxes are called phylacteries, or tephillin.

Hebrew script

CALL TO REPENTANCE

At Rosh Hashanah (the Jewish New Year), the shofar, or ram's horn, is blown to call Jewish people to repentance (to ask God to forgive all the wrong things they have done in the past year). This begins the 10 solemn days leading up to Yom Kippur, the Day of Atonement, a day of fasting and repentance, and the holiest day of the Jewish year.

Shofar (ram's horn)

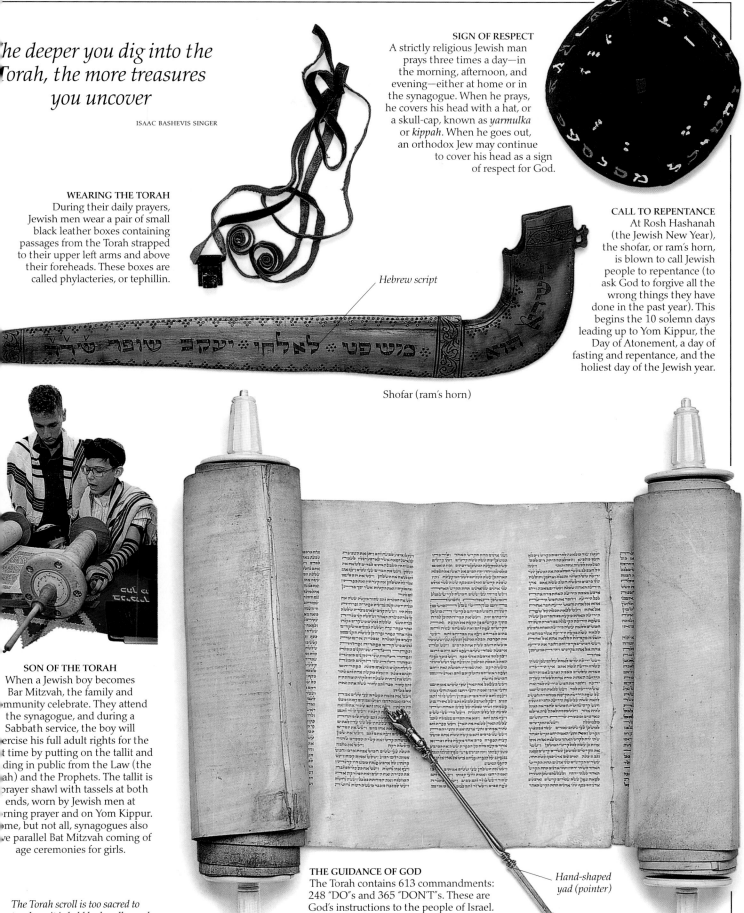

SON OF THE TORAH

When a Jewish boy becomes Bar Mitzvah, the family and community celebrate. They attend the synagogue, and during a Sabbath service, the boy will exercise his full adult rights for the first time by putting on the tallit and reading in public from the Law (the Torah) and the Prophets. The tallit is a prayer shawl with tassels at both ends, worn by Jewish men at morning prayer and on Yom Kippur. Some, but not all, synagogues also have parallel Bat Mitzvah coming of age ceremonies for girls.

The Torah scroll is too sacred to touch, so it is held by handles and a pointer is used to keep the place

THE GUIDANCE OF GOD

The Torah contains 613 commandments: 248 "DO"s and 365 "DON'T"s. These are God's instructions to the people of Israel. They express his will and are binding for religious Jews. Jews also see God's guidance expressed in the moral, physical, and religious order of the universe, and in the rules of purity and social justice with which Israel responded to God. These can also be called Torah.

Hand-shaped yad (pointer)

Family and community

THE CENTER OF JEWISH RELIGIOUS LIFE is the home. Great emphasis is placed on family and relationships. The Jewish year contains many festivals, which give a pattern and a rhythm to the community's life. Many of them are not only religious, but family festivals, too. These festivals bind the community together. They also make the continuing story of Israel's relationship with God a living part of people's lives. The most important is the weekly Shabbat (Sabbath), a day of rest when Jews do no work and recall the completion of creation. At the center of public worship and of social life is the synagogue, or "assembly." On Friday evenings and on Saturday mornings the Jewish community gathers there for Sabbath services.

Palm frond

Palm, myrtle, and willow, woven together, form the lulav

Lulav, carried in procession at Sukkot

CUP OF BLESSING
Most Jewish homes have wine goblet called a Kiddu cup. The name comes fro the words of blessing, als called Kiddush, spoken ov the wine and bread durin Sabbath and the Passove

PURIM
Nearly halfway through the Jewish year (in February or March) comes Purim, which is marked by parties where masks and elaborate costumes are sometimes worn. Purim means "lots." The name refers to a time in the 5th century BCE when an official in the Persian Empire named Haman made a plan to kill all the Jews and drew lots to decide when. During the festival the Book of Esther from the Bible is read aloud to recall how Esther, the King's wife, helped save her people from slaughter.

Purim scroll containing the Book of Esther

Etrog, a citrus fruit

SUKKOT
Sukkot takes place in September or October, at the end of harvest. During this festival Jews recall how God provided for all their needs when they wandered in the wilderness after leaving Egypt. Festive huts are built, roofed with greenery and decorated with fruit and flowers. In a ceremony called the "Four Species," followers carry a lulav (left) in procession with an etrog (above) while saying prayers.

Sukkot huts are built in gardens or next to a synagogue and, if possible, people eat and sleep in them for the week of the festival.

LIGHTING THE SABBATH CANDLES
The Jewish day begins and ends at sunset, so the Sabbath, which falls on a Saturday, begi on Friday evening, when the woman of a Jewis household kindles the "Sabbath Lights" and prays for God's blessing on her work and famil The Sabbath table is then set with bread and wine. Before the meal, the husband praises his wife and recites scriptures about creation and the Sabbath. Then he blesses the wine an bread and passes them around.

...SOVER

...week-long Passover is the best
...wn of all Jewish festivals. It is
...to commemorate the events
...ted in the Book of Exodus in
...Torah. The festival is called
...over because, when God sent
...al punishment on Egypt to
...suade Pharaoh to let his people
...the angel of death "passed
..." the Hebrews and spared
...m. At the Passover meal the
...ngest child in the family asks
...this night is different from all
...er nights. The father tells the
...y of Israel's deliverance from
...ery in Egypt (the Exodus).
...tells of the harshness of life
...gypt, of Moses who led the
...ish people out of slavery, of
...God gave Moses the Ten
...mandments, and how God
...ked after Israel in the desert.

Shankbone of lamb recalls lambs killed at the first Passover

The Haggadah (meaning "Storytelling") is the special order of service for the Passover meal

...symbolizes ...rifice

Cloth with which the unleavened bread is covered when not being eaten

The word Pesach, *Hebrew for Passover*

Nut and fruit paste

...een herb ...resenting spring

Bitter herbs to represent the bitterness of slavery

The special meal held in the home on the first two nights of Passover is called Seder (order); these dishes are placed on the table to teach the Passover story.

Matzah (bread made without yeast) recalls the haste with which the Israelites left Egypt

Salt water, as a reminder of the tears of slavery

CONTEMPLATION

To contemplate is to think about something or to gaze upon an object. Religious people practice quiet reflection and focused prayer, concentrating their minds on God, or on some other reality which transcends (rises above) the self. By this means they can experience oneness or "union" with the divine.

The Christian faith

CHRISTIANS TAKE THEIR NAME from Jesus
Christ. Jesus was a Jew who lived in the first
century in what is now Israel. At the age of 30
he gathered a band of disciples and traveled
around preaching, teaching, and healing the sick.
He declared the need for people to repent (ask for
forgiveness for their sins), and to believe and follow
him. His disciples saw Jesus as the Messiah the Jews
expected. For Christians, Jesus is not just a man.
They believe that God, creator and ruler of the
universe, became incarnate (came to Earth as
a human being) in Christ to offer forgiveness
and salvation to humankind. This was necessary,
Christians believe, because God is good and people
are not, which creates a gap or barrier between
humanity and God. Christians see Jesus as the
savior (rescuer) who brings people to God.

SIGN OF THE CROSS
Jesus was executed by being
nailed to a cross and left to die
(this is called crucifixion). The
cross later became the main
symbol of Christianity because
Christians believe that Christ
actually brought salvation by his
death and resurrection. When
people become Christians and
are baptized, they are marked
with the sign of the cross.

JOHN THE BAPTIST
At the time of Jesus's birth, many
Jews were expecting a prophet to
come as a "forerunner" heralding
the coming of the Messiah. John
began teaching before Jesus did,
preaching a baptism of repentance
for the forgiveness of sins. When
Jesus was 30, John baptized him in
the Jordan River, after which Jesus
began to teach and preach.
Christians believe that John came
to prepare the way for Jesus, and
baptism has always been the sign
of a person's entry into the
Christian community.

*The crown shows Mary
as the Queen of Heaven*

THE HOLY TRINITY
This picture is used by many Christians
to help them think about the Christian
belief that God is Trinity. This means
that there are three persons in God—
the Father, the Son, and the Holy
Spirit—yet at the same time God is
one. In the second person of the
Trinity, Jesus, God became human. In
the third person, the Holy Spirit, God
continues to be present on Earth.

VIRGIN AND CHILD
There are statues of Jesus with his
mother Mary, such as this one, in
many Christian churches. Respect
for Mary as "mother of God" has
developed steadily in some (though
not all) branches of Christianity.
She is called "the Blessed Virgin Mary"
because Christians believe that Jesus's
father was not a man, but God. Many
Christians have great reverence for Mary
and ask her to pray for them from heaven.

CHRISTIANITY

ONE GOD?
Yes: one god in three persons—
Father, Son, and Holy Spirit—
the Trinity

THE AFTERLIFE?
A final judgment, followed by
heaven or hell

FOUNDER?
Jesus Christ, who lived in Palestine
c. 6 BCE–30 CE

SCRIPTURES?
The Bible, made up of the Old
Testament (the Jewish Bible) and the
New Testament

MAJOR FESTIVALS?
Christmas—Jesus' birthday
Easter—His death and resurrection

PRIESTS?
Most churches have priests or
ministers.

THE CHRISTMAS STORY

The most familiar image of the Christian story is of Christ's nativity (birth), which Christians celebrate at Christmas. In this picture, Jesus, Mary, and her husband Joseph are surrounded by the animals who lived in the stable, local shepherds and their sheep, and angels. The angels are singing "Glory to God in the highest heaven, and on Earth peace among those whom he favors." They rejoice at the birth of Christ, the "Prince of Peace." Jesus was born at Bethlehem in Judea (southern Israel) and brought up at Nazareth in Galilee in northern Israel. His mother Mary and Joseph, although poor, were descended from Israel's most famous king, King David.

I am the light of the world. Whoever follows me will never walk in darkness but will have the light of life

JESUS IN *JOHN* 8: 12

God the Father watches from heaven, holding the world in his hand and worshiped by angels

Angels announce the birth to surprised local shepherds

Picture showing the story of Christ's birth, from a 15th-century book

The baby Jesus was born in a stable because there was no room at the inn in Bethlehem

Mary and Joseph dressed in blue, the color of divinity and heaven

The painting shows the dress and styles of the time when it was painted

Way of the cross

AT THE AGE OF THIRTY-THREE, Jesus was arrested, tortured, and crucified by the Roman authorities who then ruled Israel. Christians believe that as he died he "took on himself" the sins of everyone (all the wrong and evil that, Christians say, is in us and cuts us off from God) so that anyone could be forgiven by God and live with God forever. Three days later, according to the Bible, he rose from the dead. He appeared to and taught his disciples, then "ascended" to heaven, returning to his Father. So, for Christians, Christ is a living savior who has defeated death, he is not just a hero. They believe that he helps and guides those who follow him and that he makes it possible for all to share in his victory over death and sin.

Mary lament over the dea body of Jes

CUP OF SUFFERING
Shortly before he died, Jesus held a farewell meal, the "last supper," with his disciples. He offered them wine to drink and bread to eat and told them to drink from the cup and eat the bread ever afterward to represent his blood shed and his life laid down for them. Ever since, Christians have followed this command in services called communion services, known as the Mass, the Eucharist, or the "Lord's Supper."

MOURNING MOTH
At the beginning of the gospel story (gos means "good news"), Mary is asked if sh willing to be the mother of the Son of God, a agrees. This is seen as a great example of fai Many Christians see her as uniquely blessed God. She is not often mentioned in the Gosp but when the time came for Jesus to die she w one of the few who did not abandon him. She often pictured in Christian art. A sculpture picture showing her mourning over the de body of her son (as above) is called a pie

THE CRUCIFIXION OF CHRIST
Outside the city of Jerusalem, Jesus was put to death along with two criminals. He carried the cross on which he was to be executed to the place of his death. Crucifixion was then a common, but very painful, method of execution. Christians seek to live, to love, and to accept suffering patiently as Jesus did, following him in "the way of the cross." Pictures of the crucifixion feature greatly in Christian art. This picture shows people who were actually there, and later Christians, together at the foot of the cross, showing that all of them look to the "saving death" of Christ for their salvation.

The pelican was used as a symbol of Christ because it was believed to give up its own blood to feed its young

The writing on the cross quoted Jesus as claiming to be "King of the Jews"

One criminal taunted Jesus; the other asked "Remember me when you come into your kingdom"

John, author of the fourth Gospel, whose symbol is an eagle

ASCETICISM

The ascetic renounces or denies many ordinary human activities and bodily comforts to live a very simple, ordered, and disciplined life. Such a life also involves dedication to regular prayer and contemplation of the divine. Ascetics may even give up home and job to follow their chosen path.

E CRUCIFIX AND THE CROSS

cifixes show Christ hanging on the cross are symbols of his death and the salvation ich it is said to have brought. Crosses are pty, and so also remind Christians of his urrection. The four Gospels whose hors are represented on this cross are four books in the New Testament ich tell of the life, death, and urrection of Jesus. They are l to have been written four early Christians ed Matthew, Mark, e, and John.

Luke, author of the third Gospel, whose symbol is an ox

atthew, author of the first spel, whose symbol is a man

Lambs were traditionally used for sacrifice; Christ is pictured as the "lamb of God who takes away the sins of the world" because he sacrificed himself

If we have died with Christ, we believe that we shall also live with him

ST. PAUL, IN ROMANS 6:8

Mark, author of the second Gospel, whose symbol is a lion

RESURRECTION
The body of Jesus was laid in a tomb with a big stone across the entrance. When some of his women followers went to the tomb, they found the stone rolled away and the tomb empty. Angels appeared and told them that Jesus had risen from the dead.

ASCENSION TO HEAVEN
After his resurrection, Jesus appeared to his followers in Jerusalem and Galilee over a period of 40 days. He taught them and mmanded them to tell all people the gospel ("good news") that his death had made orgiveness and new life possible for all, and o baptize people in the name of the Father, the Son, and the Holy Spirit. Then he ascended into heaven to return to God.

The marks of the nails in Jesus' hands and feet are clearly shown in this picture of him rising from his grave

Church of Christ

CHRISTIANS BELIEVE that before Jesus ascended to heaven he promised he would send the Spirit of God to be with his followers after he left them. Shortly afterward, the Holy Spirit descended upon the disciples, who were gathered in Jerusalem, filling them with new boldness and power. They went out and preached that Jesus was the promised Messiah, calling on people to turn away from their sins and to be baptized in his name. They formed a community of faith which continues today—an assembly of baptized believers known as "the church," guided by the Holy Spirit. The early church spread rapidly from Jerusalem across the Roman Empire. Today, it numbers nearly 2 billion members worldwide. Christians see the church as "the body of Christ," united by faith in him, and called to do his work in the world. They seek to love God and other people as Jesus did, to spread his teaching, and to live as he lived.

CHURCH AND CHURCH
Christians, once baptized, make up "the church." In today's world, the church is split into a number of groups called denominations, or churches, some very large, some very small. The largest is the Roman Catholic church, which has as its head the Pope, who is based in Rome. The buildings in which Christians meet together to worship God are also called church.

THE SACRAMENT OF BAPTISM
Christians celebrate the two ceremonies of baptism and communion. These ceremonies are called sacraments (some Christians believe there are also five other sacraments). Some branches of Christianity see sacraments as signs symbolizing God's inward, spiritual work; others say they are also instruments, used by God to do that work. Baptism is the rite of entry into the church; water is used, symbolizing the spiritual cleansing of the believer's soul.

PETER THE LEADER
Peter was the first disciple to recognize Jesus as the Messiah. He became the chief of the apostles ("sent ones"), the group of 12 leading disciples, and the leader of the early Christians. He is said to have gone to Rome and led the church there.

Peter holds the keys of the kingdom of heaven

Peter is often called the "first Bishop of Rome"

Christians believe the Bible to be "the Word of God," uniquely inspired by God

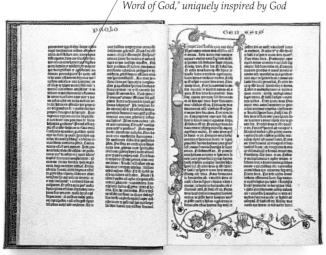

THE BIBLE
The Bible is the Christian holy book. The first part is the Jewish Bible, called the Old Testament by Christians. The second part, called the New Testament, is made up of the writings of early Christians. The Bible is seen as having unique authority.

IHS, the first three letters
of the Greek word for Jesus

As a sign of their authority, bishops
may carry a staff called a crozier,
shaped like a shepherd's crook;
this is the head of one such staff

A lamb near a cross, used to
represent the sacrifice of Christ

Martin Luther
preaching

HOPS AND SHEPHERDS

he Bible, Jesus is described as "the good
pherd." Christian leaders were therefore also
n as shepherds, called to look after the people
heir churches as a good shepherd looks after
sheep. Early Christians who led and cared
others became known as "pastors" and
ir leaders as "chief pastors" or "bishops."

ACHING AND TEACHING

us spent much of his time preaching and teaching.
stressed the importance of love and told people
orgive the sins done by others. He taught both
ermons and by parables—little stories, taken
n ordinary life, with a spiritual meaning.
best known of Jesus's sermons is the
rmon on the Mount", shown here.
us's parables and sermons are
orded in the Bible and
still used today to
h and to spread
Christian faith.

*Love the Lord your God
with all your heart…
and your neighbor
as yourself*

MARK 12:30-31

DIFFERENT CHURCHES

By the 11th century, Christianity was split into two
main groups—the Roman Catholic church in western
Europe, headed by the Pope in Rome, and the
Eastern Orthodox church, centered in Constantinople
(now Istanbul) and eastern Europe. Reformers such
as Martin Luther and John Calvin broke away from
the authority of the Pope in the 16th century, thus
creating a third main group. Their
followers came to be known
as Protestants.

The 12 apostles listen
to the sermon

Jesus Christ
preaching

The message of Islam

ISLAM IS A RELIGION of submission. Its followers, Muslims, are "those who commit themselves in surrender to the will of Allah" (Allah is the Arabic word for God). The word "Islam" itself means "commitment" or "surrender." Muslims see their faith as God's final revelation, which meets all the spiritual and religious needs of humanity. The religion was revealed to the Prophet Muhammad, who was born in the city of Mecca in Arabia, in about 571. At about the age of 40, he found that he was being called to become a prophet and preach the message of the one true God. At first, he met much opposition and in 622 he left Mecca with his followers for the nearby city of Medina. By 630, he had made them into a powerful religious and political community and was able to reenter Mecca in triumph.

THE CRESCENT
The crescent, seen on top of many mosques, originally signified the waxing moon. It is associated with special acts of devotion to God. The star and crescent appear on the flags of countries that are mainly Muslim.

SACRED TEXTS
Calligraphy (the art of writing) in Arabic is a great Islamic art. Wherever possible Muslims try to learn Arabic because God revealed his Word to Muhammad in Arabic, and they wish to read it in the original language. The writing on this tile is a fragment from the Qur'an.

The mihrab in the Gila Khalina mosque

THE KA'BAH AT MECCA
The great mosque in Mecca is built around the Ka'bah. Set into the wall of the Ka'bah is the Black Stone, which Muslims believe fell from heaven as a sign of the first covenant between God and humankind.

PILGRIMAGE TO MECCA
The Ka'bah is Islam's most sacred site. Every Muslim who is healthy, free from debt, and can afford the journey must make the pilgrimage to Mecca at least once in his lifetime, to visit the Ka'bah and other sacred sites. Pilgrimage is the fifth of the five pillars (or duties) of Islam. The others are: first, profession of faith; second, prayer; third, fasting during the month of Ramadan; and, fourth, charitable giving. The duties are based on the Qur'an, and the practices of the Prophet Muhammad.

PRAYING TOWARD MECCA
Prayer is the second of the five pillars of Islam. Muslims are required to pray five times a day, facing Mecca—in the morning, at noon, midafternoon, after sunset, and at bedtime. In every mosque there is a niche in the wall called a mihrab which faces toward Mecca to show people which way they should face as they pray.

Dome of the Rock, with its gilded dome and octagonal
e, stands in Jerusalem. After the Great Mosque at Mecca
the Prophet's tomb at Medina, it is Islam's third holiest
According to Muslim tradition, the rock at its center
the point from which the Prophet Muhammad
aculously visited heaven one night in 619. The
is also sacred to Jews and Christians, because
temples of Solomon and Herod stood here.

ISLAM	
ONE GOD?	
Yes, Allah, the merciful and compassionate	
THE AFTERLIFE?	
A last judgment, followed by heaven or hell	
FOUNDER OR PROPHET?	
The Prophet Muhammad, lived in Arabia c. 571–632	
SCRIPTURES?	
The Qur'an, revealed to Muhammad	
PRIESTS?	
None	
HOLIEST PLACE?	
The Ka'bah at Mecca in Arabia	

*The words of the shahadah are woven
into the curtain covering the
walls of the Ka'bah*

*The Ka'bah is a cubelike building made of
gray stone; the Black Stone is set into its
eastern corner, on the outside*

There is no god but God, and Muhammad is the Prophet of God

THE SHAHADAH (THE PROFESSION OF FAITH)

People of the Qur'an

Muslims believe that the Qur'an is the infallible Word of God, expressing God's will for all humankind: final, perfect, and complete. It was revealed in a miraculous way to the Prophet Muhammad, the Messenger of God, who was told to "read" or "recite" the words, which were communicated to him by the archangel Gabriel while he was in a trancelike state. Qur'an literally means "recitation." Its central teaching reveals the character of God. Next in importance, it teaches that there will be a Last Judgment, when all humanity will be raised to life and appear before God to be judged and sent to paradise or hell, depending on their behavior. It also gives much guidance for behavior here and now. Some of it was revealed in Mecca, some in Medina after Muhammad's hijra, or emigration, there in 622. Muhammad began to receive revelations from God in about 610, and continued to receive them until his death in 632. Soon after, these revelations were collected from spoken and written sources to form the Qur'an.

LEARNING TO RECITE
The Qur'an is the Muslim's constant companion. From early childhood, Muslims hear its words every day. At school, they are encouraged to learn them by heart. Often, they learn to read from passages of the Qur'an.

Believers gathered to hear a sermon being preached

PREACHING
In the mosque the minbar, or pulpit, stands to the right of the mihrab. In early times, it had only three steps, but is today often much more highly decorated and grand in scale, like the one shown here. Only the Prophet Muhammad preached from the topmost step—the imam, or teacher, must take a lower one. Muslims expect to hear a sermon read from the minbar when they gather in the mosque on Friday for noon prayers.

THE ARCHANGEL GABRIEL
When Muhammad was 40, he saw the archangel Gabriel appear before him in human form as he meditated in a cave near Mecca. The archangel spoke the words of God to him. At first, Muhammad wondered if he was imagining this, but soon he sincerely believed that he was hearing God's Word. In the role of divine messenger, he was to retell the words he heard to the Meccans, preach the existence of one God, Allah, and denounce polytheism (the worship of many gods).

THE NAMES OF GOD
The Qur'an teaches about God by giving him names that describe him, such as Great, Merciful, Keeper, or Guide. In total there are 99 such names. Muslims recite them on 33-bead rosaries, and meditate on them. Certain passages, like the famous Throneverse, surah (chapter) 2.256, inscribed here on a gemstone, describe God particularly eloquently, and at greater length.

THE QUR'AN
Muslims believe that the Qur'an is the last in a series of revelations sent to the world by God, expressing his will for humankind. The authorized version, written in incomparable classical Arabic, was prepared in about 650 CE under Uthman, the third successor to Muhammad. Muslims consider it to be perfect, and untranslatable from the original Arabic. The Qur'an has 114 surahs (chapters). It can only be touched by Muslims who have first been ceremonially cleansed.

The Qur'an is often beautifully printed and decorated and may be kept in special coverings or boxes to show how much it is valued.

O believers, believe in God and His Messenger and the Book He has sent down on His Messenger and the Book which He sent down before

QUR'AN 4.136

People of the mosque

FOR MUSLIMS, ISLAM should rule over every part of the life of a person and of a nation, without any distinction between the religious and the rest. The mosque is central to the life of the community, and mosques may be centers for education and social work. The Qur'an lays down rules to govern, not just the life of an individual, but also the life of the community. These rules cover all areas of religious and social behavior, from prayer, almsgiving, fasting, and pilgrimage, to marriage, inheritance, and food and drink. Also important are the Hadith (traditions), which record sayings and events in the life of Muhammad and the early Muslim communities. They contain the Sunnah (example) of the Prophet, the standard to which all Muslims should aspire. The Qur'an and Sunnah have combined to form the Shari'ah (law) which is a comprehensive guide to life and conduct giving a fixed code of behavior for Muslims to follow.

THE POSITIONS OF PRAYER
The above picture shows a Muslim following a fixed number of "bowings" while at prayer. There is a set sequence of movements, during which worshipers twice prostrate themselves (that is, kneel, then bow very low with their faces to the ground).

CALL TO PRAYER
Five times a day, Muslims are called to prayer by a muezzin, who cries out from a minaret (a tower in a mosque, built for this purpose). Muezzins call in Arabic, beginning "God is most great" and ending "There is no god but God!"

AT THE MOSQUE
The mosque consists of an outer courtyard with running water where worshipers perform ritual washings to prepare themselves for prayer, and a large inner area. This is usually covered in carpets and rugs, and unfurnished except for pulpit, lectern, and platform. Here people pray, and also hear a sermon at the main weekly service on Friday afternoons.

This mosque, the Badshahi mosque in Lahore, Pakistan, one of the largest in the world, can hold nearly 100,000 worshipers

Worshipers approach the mosque quietly, leave their shoes at the entrance, and ritually wash themselves

FISM
novement within
m called
ism
uses on
direct
erience of
d. Sufism
ound
hin both
nches of
m, Sunni and
'ite. Some Sufis
ce as part of
ir worship. The
cers are
ularly known
whirling
vishes."

*Compass shows
the way to Mecca*

Allahu akbar—
God is greater

CALL TO PRAYER FROM THE MINARET

PUBLIC PRAYERS
These worshipers, led
by an imam (religious
teacher), are prostrating
themselves as they pray.
As they bow they say
"Glory be to my Lord, the
great." As they prostrate
themselves they say "Glory
e to my Lord the almighty."
The megaphone ensures
that all worshipers can
hear and follow the leader.

PRAYER MAT
When Muslims pray, they face the
Ka'bah in Mecca. To find the direction
in which to pray, which is called the
qiblah, they need a special compass.
The compass is an integral part of
many modern prayer mats like the one
pictured here. Many Islamic countries,
such as Iran and Turkey, have a
tradition of weaving wonderful
carpets and prayer rugs.

*Shi'ite standard bearing
the names of God,
Muhammad, and Ali*

SUNNI AND SHI'ITE
Sunni is the majority (90 percent)
and Shi'ite the minority (10 percent)
branch of Islam. Sunni Muslims see
the Shari'ah, made by agreement of the
community, as their vital guide, and believe
that after Muhammad's death, the caliphs
(rulers) who succeeded him were his
rightful successors. Shi'ite Muslims believe
that only the descendants of Muhammad's
daughter Fatima and her husband Ali
should succeed him. They believe that after
Ali died, God sent imams, descended from
Ali, as His infallible messengers.

The modern spirit

Wɪᴛʜɪɴ ᴛʜᴇ ʟᴀsᴛ 200 years, some less familiar faiths have gained prominence—some of these, like the Church of Jesus Christ of Latter-day Saints, the Unification Family Church, and the Hare Krishna movement, are based on older disciplines, while others, such as Scientology, are completely new. Many new spiritual movements are well respected and are growing in popularity; some, however, attract criticism for their methods of recruitment and the financial workings of their organizations.

THE BAHA'I FAITH

The Baha'i religion was founded in Persia (modern Iran) in the 19th century by the prophet Bahá'u'lláh (1817–92). Over the last 150 years, the faith has grown in popularity, and there are now followers in most of the countries of the world. Bahá-u-lláh's followers, known as Baha'is, believe in one God. They stress the spiritual oneness and equality of all people. They work for world peace and social justice and believe that all the world's religions have an essential unity.

Hɪsᴛᴏʀʏ
Bahá'u'lláh was a follower of a Persian Muslim teacher called Siyyid 'Ali Muhammad Shírází, who took the title Báb ("Gate") and foretold the coming of another great religious leader, "He whom God shall make manifest." In 1863, Bahá'u'lláh claimed to be this new leader, following in a tradition of great religious figures, including Abraham, Moses, Jesus, Muhammad, and the Báb himself. After Bahá'u'lláh's death, leadership of the faith passed to his son, and then to an elected body, the Universal House of Justice.

Sᴄʀɪᴘᴛᴜʀᴇs ᴀɴᴅ ʙᴇʟɪᴇғs
Baha'i scriptures include writings of the Báb and Bahá'u'lláh, along with later texts that interpret these books. Bahá'u'lláh's *Kitáb-i-Aqdas* (Book of Laws) and *Kitáb-i-Iqán* (Book of Certitude) are two key texts. He foretells the coming of a representative of God to Earth every thousand years. These figures are not incarnations of God, but bring God's teachings to Earth in a form that is relevant to the particular age in which they appear.

Cᴏᴅᴇs ᴀɴᴅ ᴘʀᴀᴄᴛɪᴄᴇs
Every day, Baha'is pray, meditate, and study scriptures. This worship takes place in the home, in local Baha'i centers, and in seven large Baha'i Houses of Worship. There is no clergy and no set form for worship—the faith forbids rituals, except that certain prayers, called "obligatory prayers" are used on a daily basis. The faith fosters equality between men and women, and forbids such practices as gambling and intake of alcohol or drugs. Baha'is do not take part in party politics.

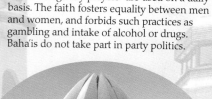

Baha'i House of Worship, known as the Lotus Temple, New Delhi, India

HARE KRISHNA

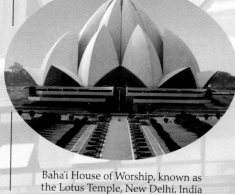

Krishna monk A. C. Bhaktivedanta Swami Prabhupada

Hare Krishna is the popular name for ISKCON (the International Society for Krishna Consciousness), part of the Hindu Vaishnava tradition.

Hɪsᴛᴏʀʏ
The movement originated in 16th-century Bengal with the saint Shri Chaitanya, who promoted *bhakti* (loving service to God), and opposed the caste system. His ideas were brought to the west in 1965 by a monk, His Divine Grace A. C. Bhaktivedanta Swami Prabhupada.

Sᴄʀɪᴘᴛᴜʀᴇs ᴀɴᴅ ʙᴇʟɪᴇғs
Krishna theology is based on the Vedas (ancient Hindu scriptures) and related texts. Followers believe in one God—Krishna—but also acknowledge lesser deities. Central to the doctrine is the idea that all living things are spiritual, but each soul, forgetting this, seeks worldly happiness, and takes on, through reincarnation, successive plant and animal bodies.

When a soul reaches the human form, the way it chooses to live determines whether it moves to a lower or higher level. If it is able to revive its love of God, it can break the cycle of birth and death and return to the spiritual realm and an eternal, blissful life of service to Krishna.

Cᴏᴅᴇs ᴀɴᴅ ᴘʀᴀᴄᴛɪᴄᴇs
ISKCON members regularly chant, study Krishna literature, and practice the system of bhakti-yoga. The saffron robes and shaven heads associated with Hare Krishna indicate young men training to be monks.

Devotees are strict vegetarians, who don't take drugs, smoke, or drink tea, coffee, or alcohol. They also abstain from gambling and sex outside marriage.

CHURCH OF JESUS CHRIST OF LATTER-DAY SAINTS

Mormon Tabernacle, Salt Lake City

Members of this Church (often called Mormons) are Christians, but they believe that after Christ and his apostles died, the Church drifted away from his doctrine. The apostle Peter prophesied that Jesus would restore his Church, and followers believe this process began in 1820 when the prophet Joseph Smith established the Church of Jesus Christ of Latter-day Saints, which follows Christ's original teachings.

HISTORY

Joseph Smith originally founded his Church in New York; he was its first president and its first prophet. After his death in 1844, he was succeeded by Brigham Young, who led the congregation to the Great Salt Lake in the present-day state of Utah. Since then, Salt Lake City has been the Church's home, and the Mormon Tabernacle there is its international center. Today, Mormon communities thrive in over 100 countries, with young missionaries regularly traveling the world to share their beliefs.

SCRIPTURES AND BELIEFS

As well as the Bible, there are three sacred Mormon texts:
* *The Book of Mormon, Another Testament of Jesus Christ*, which relates the story of Christ's visit to ancient America after the Resurrection

* *The Doctrine and Covenants*, a collection of Joseph Smith's revelations and those of his successors
* *The Pearl of Great Price*, Smith's account of founding the Church, and his translation of the record of Moses and Abraham.

Mormons believe that God has restored his Church to the Earth and that both the Bible and the *Book of Mormon* are the word of God. They also believe in the gifts of tongues, prophecy, revelation and healing, and in the eventual creation of a "New Jerusalem" in America.

Mormons see the family as the basic unit of both Church and society. For a brief time in the 19th century, polygamy was practiced by some Mormons, but it was discontinued by the Church before 1900.

CODES AND PRACTICES

The Church sets down Christian moral principles, and it particularly encourages service to others. The Mormon health code—the Word of Wisdom—forbids smoking, and drinking tea, coffee, and alcohol.

The Church allows members to be baptized after death (and even revise marriage vows so "till death us do part" becomes "for eternity"), and they are encouraged to research their ancestry in order to bring as many people as possible into the Church. To help with this, it has assembled a comprehensive genealogical archive, freely available to everyone, which is stored in granite caves in Utah.

UNIFICATION FAMILY CHURCH

Popularly known as the Moonies after their founder, the Reverend Sun Myung Moon, this organization is actually called the Holy Spirit Association for the Unification of World Christianity, or HSA-UWC. Moon's book *Divine Principle* teaches that God's original purpose was to establish perfect families that grow and multiply in a perfect relationship with him. Confounded by the fall of man, this plan is thought to have found fulfillment in the ministry of Reverend and Mrs. Moon.

HISTORY

Reverend Moon's mission was inspired by a vision of Jesus that appeared to him when he was a teenager in Korea. In 1954, he established the HSA-UWC, and he later set up a number of religious, political, media, and arts organizations to support his ministry—among these are the Summit Council for World Peace, the International Federation for Victory over Communism, and the Universal Ballet Company.

When his movement reached its 40th anniversary in 1994, Moon declared that it had reached the end of a major cycle, and the Unification Church as it was would no longer exist. Claiming that religion had run its course and God would now meet man in the family, he inaugurated the Family Federation for World Peace and Unification (FFWPU) and replaced the old Church with the new Unification Family Church.

SCRIPTURES AND BELIEFS

The Bible, the *Divine Principle*, and excerpts from Reverend Moon's sermons form Unification scriptures.

Reverend Moon sees three main problems in the world—absence of morality leading to selfcenteredness; the decline of Christianity and the lack of unity among world faiths; and the influence of God-denying doctrines, such as Communism. He believes marriage and the family to be the only path to salvation.

Unification Family Church mass wedding

CODES AND PRACTICES

Marriage, which takes the form of mass blessings, is the most important ritual in the Unification Family Church. Partners are chosen for members by Reverend Moon, although they are free to reject anyone they consider unsuitable. Couples vow to practice sexual purity and to create a family that lives according to Unification principles and contributes to world peace.

Religious timelines

These timelines provide a rough comparison of events and developments in the main religions. Because each box covers 250 years though, dates can only be approximate, and some dates—those in the life of the Buddha, for example—are unknown or disputed. More detailed information will often be found in the main section of the book.

Long-running periods, such as the Hindu Vedic period, are marked *, and the names of important writings are printed in *italic*.

Populations of World Religions

The numbers given here are approximate, and intended only as a rough comparative guide. This book does not deal with every existing religion, but extensive information about many more can be found through the websites on p. 69.

Religion	Followers	Religion	Followers
Christianity	2,100,000,000	Sikhism	23,000,000
Islam	1,600,000,000	Judaism	14,000,000
Hinduism	950,000,000	Confucianism	6,500,000
Buddhism	380,000,000	Jainism	4,200,000
Native religions	100,000,000	Shintoism	4,000,000

	2000–1750 BCE	1750–1500 BCE	1500–1250 BCE	1250–1000 BCE		750–500 BCE	500–250 BCE	250 BCE–0 CE
Ancient religions	*Egyptian Old, Middle, and New Kingdoms	Scandinavian Bronze Age	*18th Egyptian Dynasty	Zoroaster, founder of Zoroastrianism	*Fravashi*	Archaic age, Greece Early Rome	Classical Age, Greece *Early Roman Republic	*Hellenistic Age, Greece *Middle and Late Republic, Rome
Indian religions	*Indus Valley civilization		*Vedic Period	*Brahmanas* (Hindu texts)	Mahabharata War (Hindu) Parsva, 23rd Jain tirthankara	Mahavira, 24th Jain tirthankara	Epics and early *Puranas* (Hindu)	*Bhagavad Gita* (Hindu)
Buddhism			*Student Buddhist monk*		*Jain religious symbol, representing peace*		The Buddha First Council at Rajagriha	Emperor Ashoka King Milinda/ Menander Lotus Sutra
Japanese religions				*Tao Yin and Yang symbol*				
Chinese religions	*Hsia Dynasty I Ching	*Shang Dynasty		*Chou Dynasty	*T'ien-ming/ the Heavenly Mandate	*Spring— Fall period K'ung Fu-tzu (Confucius)	Lao Tzu (father of Taoism)	*Qin Dynasty *Early Han Dynasty Confucianism is State Religion
Judaism	Abraham, Isaac, and Jacob	Moses and the Exodus	Settlement in Canaan	David and the capture of Jerusalem Solomon and the Temple			Second Temple built	Temple extended Herod the Great
Christianity		*Islamic tile*						
Islam					*Catholic rosary*			

The language is mainly archaic Punjabi, but there are also passages in Sanskrit, Persian, and Khariboli

Standard versions of the Guru Granth Sahib contain 1,430 pages

GURU GRANTH SAHIB
Each religion has its own holy book, and the *Guru Granth Sahib*—also known as the Adi Granth, or primal text—is the Sikh sacred scripture. Copies must be treated with great care, so most Sikhs keep a smaller version, the *Gutka*, at home, which contains all the passages used in daily prayer.

0 CE–250 CE		500–750 CE	750–1000 CE	1000–1250 CE	1250–1500 CE	1500–1750 CE	1750–2000 CE	
Height of the Roman Empire	Emperor Augustus	Parsis settle in India			*Sikh prayer beads*		Persecution of Zoroastrians, Iran	ANCIENT RELIGIONS
Vishnu Purana *Vaishnavism *Shaivism (all Hindu)	Jain Council at Valabhi	*Vedanta age *Bhakti movement (both Hindu)	*Bhagavata Purana* (Hindu) Bahubali image and shrine (Jain)	Tantras composed		Guru Nanak Guru Gobind Singh and the *Guru Granth Sahib*	Mahatma Gandhi Partition of India Hare Krishna	INDIAN RELIGIONS
*Mahayana Buddhism Buddhism enters China	*Tibetan Buddhism Buddhism enters Korea	Buddhism enters Japan	Buddhism strong in Korea and China	Monk Eisai and Zen Buddhism	Nichiren Bayon Temple, Cambodia	Buddhism restored to Sri Lanka	Chogye Buddhism in Korea Soka Gakkai in Japan	BUDDHISM
	Founding of Ise shrine	*Nara period Buddhism in Japan declared state religion	*Kojiki* and *Nihongi* compiled (Shinto)	Dogen and Zen Buddhism	No Drama	Motoori Norinaga (Shinto scholar)	Tenrikyo religion Soka Gakkai religion	JAPANESE RELIGIONS
*Xin Dynasty Late Han Dynasty Buddhism in China	Chin Dynasty Spread of Buddhism and Taoism	*Sui Dynasty State Buddhism *Tang Dynasty	*The Five dynasties Repression of Buddhism	*Sung Dynasty Confucian revival	*Yuan Dynasty Tantric Buddhism *Ming Dynasty	*Qing Dynasty	T'ai Ping rebellion Cultural Revolution	CHINESE RELIGIONS
Temple destroyed Rabbis reconstruct Judaism			*Jewish seven-branched menorah*		Printed prayer book Expulsion from Spain	Ashkenazi and Sephardi communities develop	Hasidism and Zionism Holocaust State of Israel	JUDAISM
Jesus Peter New Testament	St. Patrick in Ireland Fall of Rome	Benedict and monasticism Augustine in England Venerable Bede	Charlemagne Orthodoxy in Russia	1st Crusade Saints Francis and Clare Cistercians/Carmelites	Dominicans Spanish Inquisition	Reformation Loyola and the Jesuits Missions to the New World	Church of J. C. of Latter-day Saints Unification Family Church	CHRISTIANITY
		Muhammad Dome of the Rock Sunni/Shi'a divide	Cordoba mosque *Sufism		*Ottoman empire Capture of Constantinople	Suleyman (Ottoman ruler) *Mughal Dynasty in India	Islamic Reform End of Caliphate Founding of Pakistan	ISLAM

Find out more

THERE ARE CENTERS OF WORSHIP for all the major religions in most towns and cities, and most are happy to provide basic information about their structure and beliefs.

For a unique cultural and historical view, however, focus on the ancient city of Jerusalem, the spiritual center of three great faiths—Christianity, Islam, and Judaism. For Christians, Jerusalem is the site of Christ's crucifixion; for Muslims, it is the place where Muhammad ascended to heaven; and for Jews, it is Zion and the City of David. Students of any of these faiths, or of religious history in general, can take in more significant sites here than anywhere else on Earth. In the nearby Holy Lands are Bethlehem, Christ's birthplace; Mount Sinai, where Moses received the Ten Commandments; and Aqaba, an important stage on the Muslim pilgrimage to Mecca.

Most faiths have similarly holy sites— the Golden Temple at Amritsar, for example, is the center of Sikhism, and the city of Varanasi is sacred to all Hindus.

MADONNA AND CHILD, BETHLEHEM
Custody of the sixth-century Church of the Nativity on the site of Christ's birth is shared by the Roman Catholic, the Armenian, and the Greek Orthodox faiths. This Madonna and Child, on view there, comes from the tradition of the Greek Orthodox church, which is responsible for the high altar in the Grotto of the Nativity, the building's spiritual heart.

Men and women worship in different areas in front of the wall.

WESTERN WALL
The plaza in front of the holy Western Wall acts as a large, open-air synagogue where Jews from all over the world gather to attend services and pray. Some visitors even write down their messages to God on pieces of paper and tuck them into the cracks between the huge, ancient stones.

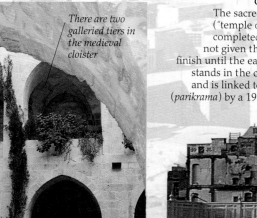

There are two galleried tiers in the medieval cloister

LUTHERAN CHURCH OF THE REDEEMER, JERUSALEM
Built for the German Kaiser Wilhelm II in 1898, the Lutheran Church of the Redeemer is situated on the remains of an 11th-century Catholic church, and its many medieval details reflect this. Shown here are the Crusader cloisters, dating from the 13th and 14th centuries and incorporated into the later building.

GOLDEN TEMPLE, AMRITSAR
The sacred Sikh shrine, or Harimandir ("temple of the Lord") at Amritsar was completed in 1601, but the walls were not given their distinctive gilded-copper finish until the early 19th century. The temple stands in the center of the lake of Amritsar and is linked to the surrounding pavement (*parikrama*) by a 196-ft (60-m) marble causeway.

VARANASI

This entire city on the banks of the holy Ganges River is believed to be a *linga*, the embodiment of the Lord Shiva, as well as his home. The river's waters are considered to be especially purifying here and Hindus believe that anyone who dies in Varanasi will go straight to heaven, whatever they have done or whatever they believe.

USEFUL WEBSITES

• Kid's site with information about religion. Look for the section where questions about religion are answered by experts:
http://kids.yahoo.com/directory/School-Bell/Social-Studies/Religion

• General site that offers an objective overview of six religions—Islam, Hinduism, Christianity, Buddhism, Judaism, and Sikhism:
http://www.bbc.co.uk/religion/religions/

• Directory of Web sites for a wide range of religious organizations:
http://www.wabashcenter.wabash.edu/resources/guide-headings.aspx

• General site that provides independent surveys of more than 4,200 religions, including statistics, research data, and membership information: **www.adherents.com**

• Survey of sacred places associated with various cultures and religions:
www.sacredsites.com

Statue of Parvati, wife of Shiva, at Varanasi

Places to visit

CHRISTIAN JERUSALEM

Dominating the holy city from the Christian perspective is the Church of the Holy Sepulcher, which encompasses the rock of Golgotha where Christ was crucified, and, most sacred of all, his tomb. Also of interest are the Church of St. John the Baptist, associated with the Crusader Knights, and the Lutheran Church of the Redeemer with its medieval cloister.

JEWISH JERUSALEM

The Western, or Wailing, Wall, in the Old City is Judaism's holiest place; a center of pilgrimage, it is all that is left of the great Temple, built to hold the Ark of the Covenant. A few streets away are the Wohl Architectural Museum, with its remains of Jewish houses from the time of Herod the Great, and the four Sephardic Synagogues, two of which date from the 17th century. (Sephardic Jews are those of Spanish or Portuguese descent).

MUSLIM JERUSALEM

Dominating the city architecturally is the stunning Dome of the Rock, designed and built to express the glory of Islam; next to it is the much smaller Dome of the Chain with its superb 13th-century tiling. The main center of Islamic worship in Jerusalem, however, is the El-Aqsa Mosque, originally built in the early 8th century.

GOLDEN TEMPLE, AMRITSAR, INDIA

The spiritual center of Sikhism, the Golden Temple (named for its gleaming facade) is a living symbol of the faith's spiritual and historical traditions. Included in its architecture, for example, are images associated with other religions, put there to express the Sikh spirit of tolerance.

VARANASI, INDIA

The most important pilgrimage site in the Hindu faith, Varanasi is also known as Kashi, the City of Light, and, since the period of British rule, as Benares. Pilgrims make offerings to shrines all along the banks of the sacred Ganges River, which is worshiped by Hindus as the river goddess Ganga.

JAIN TEMPLE, KOLKATA, INDIA

The temple complex, at Sitambar, Kolkata, is dedicated to the tenth Tirthankara (conqueror), Shitala, whose image is at its center; in all, there are believed to be 24 Tirthankaras, who teach and guide mortal souls. Although Jains do not officially worship gods, minor Hindu deities adorn the entrance. The building itself is very elaborate, since—like all Jain temples—it is intended to be a replica of the celestial assembly halls.

Twentieth Tirthankara

Glossary

Christian angel

AFTERLIFE Life after death.

AHIMSA The principle of not inflicting harm on other living things, which is central to the Jain and Hindu faiths.

ANGEL Divine messenger; attendant spirit.

ANKH Ancient Egyptian symbol of life, which only gods and royalty carried.

APOSTLE Literally "sent one" or "messenger"; one of the 12 men Jesus sent into the world with his message.

ASCETIC Someone who practices extreme self-denial and self-discipline, usually for the purpose of spiritual enlightenment. Ascetics often spend their lives in regular prayer and contemplation.

AUM The eternal syllable, sacred to Hindus. It is chanted or sung before and after prayers.

BAPTISM Religious ceremony involving immersion in, or sprinkling with, water as a sign of purification, or admission to a particular church. Baptism is often accompanied by name-giving.

Christian baptism shown in a Viking illustration

BAR MITZVAH Initiation ceremony for Jewish boys entering adulthood. Bar Mitzvah means "son of the commandment."

BAT MITZVAH Initiation ceremony for Jewish girls entering adulthood. Bat Mitzvah means "daughter of the commandment."

BIBLE Scriptures of the Old and New Testament in Christianity; also used to refer to the scriptures of other religions. (*see also* TESTAMENT)

CHURCH Building used for public Christian worship; collective expression for all Christians; organized Christian body (Church of Scotland, Church of Jesus Christ of Latter-day Saints, etc.).

CREATION Act of creating the world; all created things—animate and inanimate.

CRESCENT Shape representing the Moon in its first or last quarter, which is the symbol of Islam.

CROSS Symbol of Jesus Christ's crucifixion, and emblem of the Christian faith. (*see also* CRUCIFIXION)

CRUCIFIXION Ancient method of execution that involved nailing a condemned person to a cross and leaving him to die; image of Jesus Christ's crucifixion.

DEITY God—either single (as in Christianity), or one of a number (as in the religions of ancient Egypt or Rome).

DEMON Evil spirit or devil; destructive supernatural being.

DENOMINATION Religious group or sect. (*see also* SECT)

DISCIPLE Follower or adherent of a religious leader.

DOCTRINE Body of religious (or scientific, or political) belief.

FRAVASHI Guardian spirit in Zoroastrianism; fravashis represent the good, or the essence of God, in everyone.

GOSPEL Teachings of Jesus Christ; record of Christ's teachings in the first four books of the New Testament: Matthew, Mark, Luke, and John; one of these books.

GURDWARA Sikh temple; the word means "the door of the guru."

GURU GRANTH SAHIB Sikh holy scriptures, which contain spiritual poetry written by the ten human gurus.

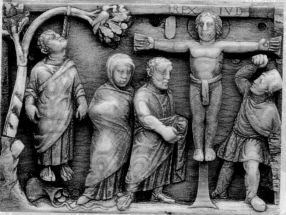

Detail of a carved ivory box from ancient Rome that depicts the crucifixion of Jesus Christ.

HERETIC Someone who holds an opinion that contradicts religious doctrine.

IDEOLOGY Manner of thinking; ideas at the basis of a particular system.

IMAM Muslim teacher or prayer leader.

IMMORTAL Able to live forever; incorruptible; unfading.

INCARNATION Process by which a god takes on bodily—often human—form.

KAMI Gods or supernatural spirits in the Shinto faith. Nature, which is seen as divine, is also called kami.

KARMA Sum of a person's actions in one life, which, according to Hindu and Buddhist doctrines, decide his or her fate in the next life.

Hindu naga

LAMA Priest in the religions of Tibetan or Mongolian Buddhism.

MANDIR Hindu temple or place of worship.

MANTRA Devotional song or chant, usually repeated many times, that is particularly associated with Hindu and Buddhist rituals.

MEDITATION Religious contemplation that involves freeing the mind of all distracting thoughts.

MIHRAB Niche in the wall of a mosque, used to show the direction of Mecca.

MINBAR Pulpit in a mosque, which stands to the right of the mihrab.

MOKSHA Salvation in the form of release from the cycle of rebirth and reincarnation.

MONOTHEISM Belief that there is only one God.

MORALITY System of principles, ethics and conduct; the degree to which such a system is followed.

MOSQUE Muslim place of worship.

NAGA Semi-human sacred snake in Hindu mythology.

NIRVANA In Hinduism and Buddhism, the state of perfect peace and happiness achieved by conquering individuality and desire and gaining freedom from karma. (*see also* KARMA)

NISHAN SAHIB Emblem of the Sikh faith, consisting of a ring of steel and a two-edged sword, with two crossed, curved swords around the outside.

POLYGAMY The practice of having more than one wife (or, less frequently, husband) at one time.

POLYTHEISM Worship of many gods rather than one God.

PROPHECY Foretelling of future events.

PROPHET Divinely inspired teacher or interpreter of God's Word; someone who foretells future events.

PUJA Hindu rite of daily worship.

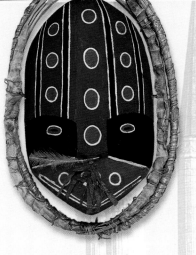

Shaman's mask from Alaska

RELIC Part of a holy person's body, or item belonging to a holy person, which is kept after death as an object of reverence.

RESURRECTION Miraculously rising up from a state of death.

RITUAL Concerned with religion; set order of performing religious rites.

SABBATH Religious day of rest.

SACRAMENT Religious ceremony or rite that symbolizes an inner spiritual state; baptism, marriage, and communion are all sacraments.

SACRIFICE Killing of a living thing, or surrender of a pleasure or possession, as an offering to a god or gods.

SADHU Wandering holy man, sage, or ascetic in India. (*see also* ASCETIC)

SARCOPHAGUS Elaborate and massive outer stone coffin.

SCRIPTURE Sacred religious book or collection of writings.

SECT Group of people who follow a particular religious doctrine, different from that of the established church from which they have separated.

SHAMAN Priest or witch-doctor who is able to contact the spirit world.

Roman sarcophagus

QUR'AN The word of God as revealed to prophet Muhammad, making up the sacred scriptures of Islam.

REBIRTH Spiritual awakening, passing from childhood to adulthood, or moving from death to life; often symbolized by immersion in, or sprinkling with, water.

REINCARNATION The belief that we live many different lives on Earth, each soul moving into another body after death.

SHRINE Altar or chapel with special religious associations; casket, especially one holding sacred relics.

SOUL Spiritual part of a person that survives bodily death.

STAR OF DAVID Figure of two interlaced equilateral triangles that symbolize the Jewish faith.

STUPA Round, often domed, mound or building used as a Buddhist shrine.

SUPPLICATION Act of making a humble request to a god or person.

SYNAGOGUE Jewish place of meeting for religious observance and instruction; Jewish assembly or congregation.

TEMPLE Building dedicated to the worship of a god (or gods) or to any other object of reverence; place is which God is believed to reside.

TESTAMENT Statement of principles and beliefs.

THEOLOGY Study of religion; rational analysis of religious faith.

TOMB Grave, monument, or building where the body of a dead person is laid to rest.

TONGUES Unknown languages, especially those that are uttered spontaneously as part of a religious experience or a service of worship.

TORAH The Law of Moses, written in the first five books of the Hebrew Bible, traditionally on scrolls with decorative ends or finials; the word "Torah" means teaching and guidance as well as law.

TRANSMIGRATION The journey of the soul from one life to the next in the process of reincarnation. (*see also* REINCARNATION)

TRINITY The Christian concept of one God who exists as three entities or persons—the Father, the Son, and the Holy Spirit.

UNDERWORLD In many ancient religions, the place deep under the surface of the Earth where the dead live.

VEDAS Early Hindu holy scriptures that are made up of four collections of text. The Vedas, which were originally transmitted orally, are believed to contain eternal truths.

YIN-YANG Symbol of Taoism consisting of a circle divided into light and dark segments by a curved line. This symbol represents the two opposite and complementary halves of the Tao, or natural force.

Jewish Torah scrolls

Index

Acknowledgments

Dorling Kindersley would like to thank:
The Ashmolean Museum (Andrew Topsfield); Surinder Singh Attariwala; The British Museum (Richard Blurton, Dylan Jackson, Graham Javes, Chris Kirby, Jane Newsom); The Buddhapadipa Temple (Venerable Phrakru Lom); The Central London Gurdwara (Bhupinder Bhasin Singh); David and Barbara Farbey; Glasgow Museums (Patricia Bascom, Jim Dunn, Ellen Howden, Antonia Lovelace, Mark O'Neil, Winnie Tyrell); Golders Green United Synagogue (Philip Solomons); Dr Ian L. Harris, Principal Lecturer in Religious Studies, University College of St. Martin, Lancaster; Professor John Hinnells, Professor of Comparative Religion, School of Oriental and African Studies, University of London; Dora Holzhandler; The Jewish Museum, London (Alisa Jaffa); New World Aurora, Neal's Yard, Covent Garden; The Powell-Cotton Museum, Birchington, Kent (Derek and Sonja Howlett, Malcolm Harman); Dr. John Shepherd, Reader in Religious Studies, University College of St Martin, Lancaster; Indarjit Singh; K. S. Singh; Westminster Cathedral (Father Mark Langham); The Zoroastrian Trust Funds of Europe (Incorporated) (Rusi Dalal). **Artwork:** Sallie Alane Reason; **Proofreading** Caitlin Doyle; **Index** Helen Peters; **Additional photography:** Janet Peckham at the British Museum.

The publisher would like to thank the following for their kind permission to reproduce their photographs:
(Key: a-above; b-below/bottom; c-center; f-far; l-left; r-right; t-top)
akg-images: De Agostini Pict.Lib. 11l; **The American Museum of Natural History**, New York (Cat. No. 16/1507): 17bl. **Ancient Art & Architecture Collection:** 55tr; **A.S.A.P.** / **Gadi Geffen:** 46bl. **Andes Press Agency:** Carlos Reyes-Manzo 64tl; Peter Grant 64–65 background. **Ashmolean Museum, Oxford:** 53tl. **Bridgeman Art Library**, London /Victoria and Albert Museum, London 21tl, / Bibliotheque Nationale, Paris 30tl, / British Library 36tl, 52br, / Giraudon / **Musée Condée, Chantilly** Front Cover c & 49l, / **Oriental Museum, Durham University** 25r, / Osma-Soria Chapter House, Soria / Index 51bl / Staatliche Museen, Berlin 13tl, / **Staats-und Universitatsbibliothek**, Hamburg 42tl, / Tretyakov Gallery, Moscow 48c. **British Library:** 52bl, Back Cover bl & 56l. **British Museum:** 4c, 10–11b, 10tr, 10c, 10tl, 11c, 11tl, 11cl, 12br, 12tl, Front Cover bc & 57tl; 68br, 70bc. **Central London Gurdwara:** 69t. **Corbis:** Bettmann 16c, Werner Forman 17tl, Ted Spiege / Terra 17cl, Ruggero Vanni 14bl; **Alistair Duncan:** 66bl, 66–67background, 71cl. **E.T. Archive** / **National Museum of Denmark** 7tr. **Mary Evans Picture Library:** 20tr, 31bcl, 58tr. **Werner Forman Archive:** 8tr, 34tr; Photographie Giraudon /

Musée Condée, Chantilly 57br, / Musée Guimet, Paris 24br. **Gables:** 67c. **Getty Images:** Richard Ashworth / Robert Harding World Imagery 17tc, Dea / A. Dagli Orti / De Agostini 14tl, Dea / A. Jemolo / De Agostini Picture Library 10tr, Dea / G. Dagli Orti / De Agostini Picture Library 15l, Dea / G. Dagliorti / De Agostini 10tl, Dea / G. Dagliorti / De Agostini Picture Library 11br, Dea / S. Vannini / De Agostini Picture Library 10c, Dea Picture Library / De Agostini Picture Library 14c, Leemage / Universal Images Group 15clb; **Glasgow Museums:** 67br, 70cr, 71tc; **The Burrell Collection:** 13l, 31br, Back Cover tl & 51br, / St Mungo Museum of Religious Life & Art 15r, © Dora Holzhandler 46br; **Sally & Richard Greenhill** / **Sam Greenhill:** 28tl. **Sonia Halliday Photographs:** 12tr, 42c. **Robert Harding Picture Library:** 8tl, 9tl, 16tr, 22tl, 22bl, 26cr, 26tl, 34tl, 38rc, 44tr, 52tr, 54c, 59c. **Hutchison Library:** 14c, / **Nick Haslam** 29bl, / **Emile Salmanov** 41tr, / **Michael MacIntyre** 35tr. **Images Colour Library:** 32bl. **Impact:** / Christopher Cormack 38lc, / G. Mermet / Cedri 25tr, / **Mohamed Ansar** 22tr. **Jewish Museum:** 71br. **Joods Historisch Museum, Amsterdam:** 44tl; **Magnum** / **Abbas:** 56tr, / **Bruno Barbey** 8br, 40rc, 40lc, / **Fred Mayer** 33br. **Nelson-Atkins Museum of Art, Kansas City, Missouri (Gift of Bronson Trevor in honour of his father, John Trevor):** 30tr. **Christine Osborne:** 64bl, 66tr, 66–67b, 67tl. **Panos Pictures** / **Paul Smith:** 52cl. **Ann & Bury Peerless:** 37bl, Front

Cover lac & 39tl, 58–59b. **Pitt Rivers Museum, Oxford:** 32–33b. **Popperfoto:** 64cl. Reuters 65br. **Peter Sanders:** 54–55b, 54bl, 58tl, 66ca. **Scala:** Florence / Bargello, Florence 48tr, / Museo di S. Marco, Florence 50b, 53br, / St Peter's, The Vatican, Rome 50tr. **Tony Souter:** 70–71background. **Spectrum Colour Library:** 34bl. **Frank Spooner Pictures:** 20tl, Bartholome / Liaison 37tl; **Museum of the Order of St John:** 50tl. **Tony Stone Images** / **Patrick Ward:** 8–9c. **Topham Picture Source:** 30bl. **Trip** / **H. Rogers:** 38tl. **ZEFA Pictures:** 45cl

Wall chart
Christophe Boisvieux / Terra clb, Angelo Cavalli / zefa bl, Arte & Immagini srl / Value Art cr; **Dorling Kindersley:** Bolton Museum and Archive Service tc, Central London Gurdwara fbl, Danish National Museum fcla, Powell-Cotton Museum, Kent ca, cla, bc, St Mungo, Glasgow Museums fcr; **Getty Images:** AFP fbr

Jacket credits: Front: **Corbis:** Bill Ross c; **Dorling Kindersley:** Ashmolean Museum, Oxford tr, Glasgow Museums—DK Images tl, tc, ftl, Powell-Cotton Museum, Kent ca; Back: **The Bridgeman Art Library:** British Library Board tr; **Dorling Kindersley:** Glasgow Museums—DK Images clb, c, Powell-Cotton Museum, Kent tl

All other images © Dorling Kindersley.
For further information, see: **www.dkimages.com**